Prepare for Social Security

WORKBOOK

THE INSIDER'S GUIDE® TO MAXIMIZING YOUR RETIREMENT BENEFITS

Matt Feret

Prepare
for Social
Security

WORKBOOK

THE INSIDER'S GUIDE® TO MAXIMIZING
YOUR RETIREMENT BENEFITS

Matt Feret

LOOKING FOR A TRUSTED ADVISOR?

Looking for Help With Social Security, IRMAA, or Medicare?

If you're reading this book, you're already doing something smart—learning how Social Security works before making decisions that can affect your income for the rest of your life.

What many people often don't realize at first is how closely Social Security and Medicare are connected.

You enroll in Medicare through Social Security. The timing of when you claim Social Security can affect when and how you enroll in Medicare. And income decisions tied to Social Security can directly affect Medicare premiums through income-related monthly adjustment amounts, commonly known as IRMAA.

Because of this overlap, it's common for Social Security questions to lead to IRMAA questions—and eventually Medicare questions as well.

If you want one-on-one help with Social Security decisions—including claiming strategies, timing, coordination with other income, or appeals, I work with a trusted Social Security consulting partner. You can find education and consulting options at:

PrepareforSocialSecurity.com

If IRMAA applies to you, or you believe you're being charged too much for Medicare premiums due to income, I also work with a specialized IRMAA consulting partner who focuses specifically on IRMAA analysis and appeals. You can learn more here:

PrepareforMedicare.com/IRMAA

If you want personal help choosing or managing Medicare coverage, the person I trust most is my wife, Niki. She is the founder and president of Brickhouse Agency, a boutique Medicare insurance agency serving clients across most U.S. states. Her team focuses on education first, clear explanations, and helping people understand how Medicare fits into the bigger picture of retirement decisions.

You can schedule a no-cost Medicare consultation (no obligation to enroll) at:

BrickhouseAgency.com

These resources are optional and educational. You don't need to use them to continue working through this book—but they're available if you want personalized guidance beyond what's covered here.

Brickhouse Agency is an independent insurance agency. Consultations are free, and there is no obligation to enroll. Brickhouse Agency is not connected with or endorsed by the U.S. government or the federal Medicare program.

Social Security and IRMAA consulting services referenced are provided by independent third parties. Any compensation received does not increase your costs and does not influence the educational content of this book.

TABLE OF CONTENTS

SPECIAL INVITATION

Please note that Social Security rules, regulations, policies, and benefits are subject to change. If you'd like to get the most up-to-date information, find the nearest Social Security office near you, view the "Helpful Links" section, sign up for my newsletter, or download free helpful checklists referenced in the book, join us at https://PrepareforSocialSecurity.com.

INTRODUCTION

Hello! I'm Matt—thanks for picking up this workbook.

I write books, create courses, and produce educational content that helps adults, retirees, and caregivers make smart, confident decisions about Social Security, Medicare, and retirement planning

I've worked inside the insurance and retirement benefits industry since 2001, and I still learn something new every week. It doesn't matter whether you have a GED or a Ph.D.—Social Security and Medicare are confusing for everyone. The rules change, the timelines matter, and these programs directly affect your income, healthcare, and financial security.

That's why I created the *Prepare for Social Security*® and *Prepare for Medicare*® series, and why I update them periodically. They're designed to give you clear insight, insider context, and practical strategies—not sales pitches.

This workbook is meant to be a hands-on companion to the book. Inside, you'll find worksheets, prompts, and exercises to help you organize information, think through scenarios, and prepare for real-world Social Security decisions.

I've also built online hubs with guides, checklists, videos, worksheets, and practical tools to help you make confident Social Security and Medicare decisions. If you want education, you'll find it there. If you want one-on-one help, both sites can connect you with licensed professionals and trusted resources I know and respect.

You can find everything at:

PrepareforSocialSecurity.com

PrepareforMedicare.com

I also host *The Matt Feret Show*, a podcast and YouTube channel focused on the health, wealth, and wellness of adults navigating midlife and beyond. I speak with insiders, authors, researchers, doctors, and professionals who help bring clarity to the decisions that truly matter.

If you want ongoing insights beyond this workbook, I publish a free newsletter that covers retirement decisions people actually face—Social Security, Medicare, healthcare costs, income planning, work-after-65 questions, and the real tradeoffs that show up as life changes. It's written for adults 50+ who want clarity, not hype, and it focuses on what's changing, what matters, and how the pieces fit together.

Here's to your wealth, wisdom, and wellness—and to making smarter decisions, together.

—matt feret

Matt Feret

WEBSITES & RESOURCES

The following websites provide additional education, tools, and optional support related to the topics covered in this workbook. They are designed to complement—not replace—the information here.

PrepareforSocialSecurity.com

Education, articles, tools, and optional consulting resources focused on Social Security claiming, timing decisions, income coordination, consulting services and appeals.

PrepareforMedicare.com/IRMAA

Education and consulting resources focused specifically on IRMAA, including how Medicare premiums are affected by income and when appeals may apply.

BrickhouseAgency.com

Medicare education and plan assistance provided by Brickhouse Agency, an independent insurance agency founded by Niki Feret. Consultations are free, with no obligation to enroll.

TheMattFeretShow.com

Long-form conversations, articles, and videos exploring health, wealth, work, relationships, and the decisions adults face in midlife and beyond.

Additional books by the author, including titles focused on Medicare and working past age 65, can be found wherever books are sold.

★   ★   ★   ★   ★

If you are just now starting to think about Social Security, or even if you have been making plans for a while, you may want to consider filling out an Authorization Form (Consent for Release of Information) to allow family or friends to contact the Social Security Administration on your behalf. You must give prior permission, in writing, for someone to be given access to your personal information. You can "revoke permission" or change the individual listed as authorized later if you like. It's important to make sure you take care of this before it's needed. You can find the authorization form by visiting https://PrepareforSocialSecurity.com/links.

You should fill it out online, print it, and either mail it or bring it to your local Social Security office, which you can find by visiting https://SocialSecurity.gov.

★   ★   ★   ★   ★

This workbook will guide you through the following:

1. Social Security basics, including a summary of your benefits and how to file.

2. Some considerations for deciding when to file.

3. How to file by DIY (Do-It-Yourself).

4. How to identify a consultant or advisor who can help you file.

THIS WORKBOOK HAS FOUR SECTIONS

SECTION ONE: PREPARE INITIALLY—DISCOVERING YOUR OPTIONS

This section is meant for people who are new to the basic concepts of Social Security, or who will be eligible for Social Security soon. It summarizes what Social Security is, what kinds of benefits you can expect and how they are calculated, and how to file for social security. We'll provide you with different ways to contact the SSA and different ways to complete your application.

SECTION TWO: PREPARE TO CHOOSE—MAKING YOUR BIG DECISION

In this section, we will guide you through some considerations and options for choosing when to file for Social Security, including: determining your benefit amount, deciding when to claim your benefits, whether or not you should use the break-even strategy, the "double-whammy effect" of Social Security taxation, survivors benefits, Social Security exemptions, different life situations that can impact your retirement strategy, whether you should keep working while drawing benefits, how to read your Social Security statement, and steps to consider when making your decision.

SECTION THREE: PREPARE TO FILE—DOING IT YOURSELF (DIY)

In this section, we will guide you through the process of filing for Social Security if you are going through the process on your own. We'll help you decide whether or not to use a DIY strategy, how to file your application, determine your benefit amount, determine whether or not you will need to pay taxes on your benefits, how to appeal a decision by the SSA you disagree with, understand how to claim survivors benefits, know how to file for Social Security benefits, and navigate the system with some general advice.

SECTION FOUR: PREPARE TO FILE—USING A CONSULTANT OR ADVISOR

In this section, we will guide you through the process of filing for Social Security if you are using a consultant or advisor. We'll talk you through the pros and cons of using an advisor rather than doing it yourself. You'll also find a checklist to help you identify reputable advisors and a list of red flags that tell you to run the other way! We'll also help you prepare for your first appointment with an advisor and know what to expect.

NOTES:

....

....

....

....

....

....

....

....

....

....

....

....

....

....

....

....

....

....

....

MY PERSONAL
SOCIAL SECURITY INFORMATION

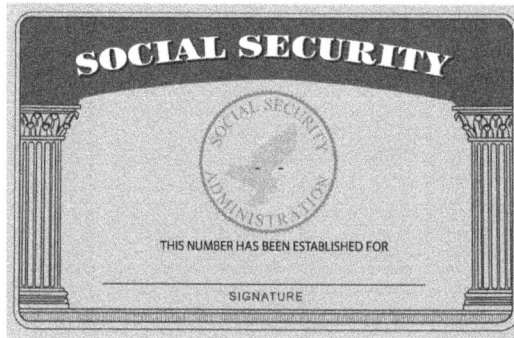

SOCIAL SECURITY

THIS NUMBER HAS BEEN ESTABLISHED FOR

SIGNATURE

MY INFORMATION

Full legal name: ....

Social Security number: ....

Date of birth: ....

Place of birth: ....

Citizenship status: ....

Beginning date of pre-1968 military service: ....

Ending date of pre-1968 military service: ....

MY SPOUSE'S INFORMATION

Full legal name: ....

Social Security number: ....

Date of birth: ....

Place of birth: ....

Date of marriage: ....

Place of marriage: ....

Date of death: ....

MY EX-SPOUSE'S INFORMATION

Full legal name: ....

Social Security number: ....

Date of birth: ....

Place of birth: ....

Date of marriage: ....

Place of marriage: ....

Date of divorce: ....

Date of death: ....

MY CHILDREN'S INFORMATION
NAMES OF CHILDREN 18 OR YOUNGER

....

....

....

....

NAMES OF CHILDREN ENROLLED IN ELEMENTARY OR SECONDARY SCHOOL:

....

....

NAMES OF CHILDREN DISABLED BEFORE AGE 22:

....

....

MY CURRENT AND LAST YEAR'S EMPLOYER(S)

Employer 1 Name: ....

Employer 1 Address: ....

Employer 2 Name: ....

Employer 2 Address: ....

Employer 3 Name: ....

Employer 3 Address: ....

MY FINANCIAL INFORMATION

My bank: ....

Bank routing number: ....

My account number: ....

Current year income: ....

Last year's income: ....

Estimated income next year: ....

MY ANSWERS TO SOCIAL SECURITY QUESTIONS:

Have you or someone on your behalf ever filed for Social Security benefits, Medicare, or Supplemental Security Income?

....

Have you ever used any other Social Security number?

....

What month do you want your Social Security retirement benefits to begin?

....

If you are within three months of age 65, do you want to enroll in Medical Insurance (Part B of Medicare)?

....

Have you become unable to work because of illnesses, injuries, or conditions at any time within the past 14 months? If so, what is the date you became unable to work?

....

....

....

....

Have you or your spouse ever worked in the railroad industry?

....

Have you earned Social Security credits under another country's Social Security system?

....

Do you qualify for or expect to receive a pension or annuity based on your employment with the federal government of the United States or one of its states or local subdivisions?

....

....

....

MY DOCUMENTS

☐ Birth certificate (original or certified copy)

☐ W-2 earnings statements and/or self-employment tax return from the previous year (photocopies are okay)

☐ Military discharge papers, e.g., DD-214 Certificate of Release or Discharge from Active Duty (photocopies are okay)

☐ Proof of U.S. citizenship or lawful alien status (original or certified copies) if you were not born in the United States

☐ A copy of your Social Security Statement or your earnings record
(If you do not have a Statement, you can view your Social Security Statement online by creating an account and signing in.)

SECTION ONE:

PREPARE INITIALLY— DISCOVER YOUR OPTIONS

This section is meant for people who are new to the basic concepts of Social Security, or who will be eligible for Social Security soon.

WHAT IS SOCIAL SECURITY?

Social Security is a social insurance program that partially replaces earnings lost to retirement, disability, or death for workers and their families. It is administered by the United States government and funded jointly by contributions from workers and employees. It provides reliable retirement income, disability benefits, and survivors benefits to spouses and children of deceased workers.

Social Security can help in far more ways than the average person realizes. For example, did you know that there are many different ways a married couple can claim Social Security benefits, depending on timing, earnings history, spousal and survivor rules, and individual circumstances (source: https://PrepareforSocialSecurity.com/sources)?

The program began in 1935 to help mitigate the severe effects of the Great Depression, two years after unemployment had reached an all-time high of almost 25%. People's life savings were wiped out, and half the senior population lived in poverty. The program was gradually expanded over the years to provide more benefits and cover more categories of workers (source: https://PrepareforSocialSecurity.com/sources).

Social Security provides the lion's share of the income for most older Americans. For about 25% of seniors, Social Security provides 90% or more of their income. So, chances are high that Social Security will make up a large chunk, if not the majority, of your income as a retiree (source: https://PrepareforSocialSecurity.com/sources).

Today only 76% of those who receive Social Security are retired workers. The remainder are survivors, children, or disabled workers. More than $1 trillion of the program's funding comes through payroll taxes. Employers and employees each pay 6.2% of earnings, and those who are self-employed pay the full 12.4% themselves. A further $108 billion of the program's funding comes from interest earnings and taxation of Social Security benefits (source: https://PrepareforSocialSecurity.com/sources).

Social Security ran a surplus every year from 1982 to 2020 but began running a deficit in 2021. This was due not only to the financial shock of the COVID-19 pandemic but because of the long-term demographic challenge of an aging population. The Baby Boomers are a very large cohort of the population who had relatively few children. Combined with lengthened lifespans, this means the American population overall is aging rapidly. In 1945 there were 41.9 workers paying into the program for each retiree receiving benefits; today, that number is only 2.8 workers per retiree (source: https://PrepareforSocialSecurity.com/sources)!

It is estimated that Social Security can continue paying full benefits until its trust fund is depleted in the coming decade. After that, the program is expected to continue paying a substantial portion of scheduled benefits through ongoing tax income. After that, it will continue to pay about 80% of benefits indefinitely through tax income. Reforms such as tax increases, benefit reductions, alternative investment plans, or growing the taxpaying workforce through immigration are possible ways to close the funding gap and avoid cutting benefits. Due to the political sensitivity of this issue, Congress is unlikely to take action on it until it becomes unavoidable (source: https://PrepareforSocialSecurity.com/sources).

Most analysts agree, though, that people currently receiving benefits or nearing the point of retirement will be gradually included in existing benefit levels and will not have to worry about a major reduction in their benefits.

The Social Security system itself has some genuine strengths that give us legitimate reasons for optimism:

- It is backed by the United States government and powerful political interests.
- It reliably pays monthly benefits to qualified retirees and the disabled.
- It gives you the flexibility to decide when to retire so that you can adjust your benefits to your family situation.
- It supports low-income workers based on years of work rather than their income level.
- It provides non-working married people with a benefit of 50% of their working spouse's benefit. This benefit is also available to divorced spouses.
- It allows you to continue working during retirement to supplement your income if you choose.

- It provides for you, your spouse, and your dependents in the event of your death or disability.

- It provides inflation-adjusted monthly payments, guaranteed for life.

That said, if you are intentional about your Social Security choices and plan correctly with the help of responsible financial advisors and books like this one, you don't need to be intimidated by the bureaucracy. Millions of people have navigated this system before you, and millions more will after you. You can do it too.

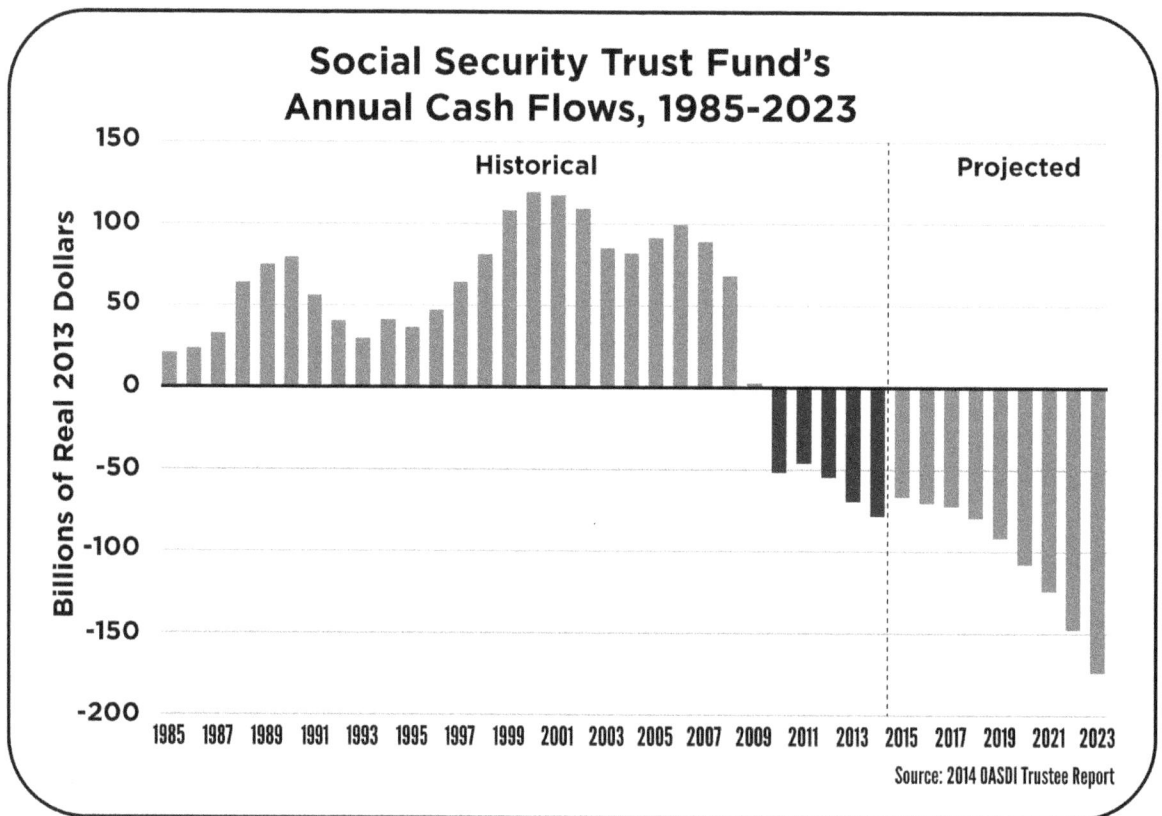

Social Security Trust Fund's Annual Cash Flows, 1985-2023

Source: 2014 OASDI Trustee Report

Source: https://www.mercatus.org/publications/social-security/update-social-security-remains-unsustainable-path

Social Security Revenue and Cost

($ Millions)

Payroll Taxes   Income From Taxing Benefits   General Fund Reimbursement   Net Interest

Total Cost

$1,200,000

$1,000,000

$800,000

$600,000

$400,000

$200,000

$0

1957 1958 1959 1960 1961 1962 1963 1964 1965 1966 1968 1969 1970 1971 1972 1973 1974 1975 1976 1977 1978 1979 1980 1981 1982 1983 1984 1985 1987 1988 1989 1990 1991 1992 1993 1994 1995 1996 1997 1998 1999 2000 2001 2002 2003 2004 2005 2006 2007 2008 2009 2010 2011 2012 2013 2014 2015 2016 2017 2018 2019

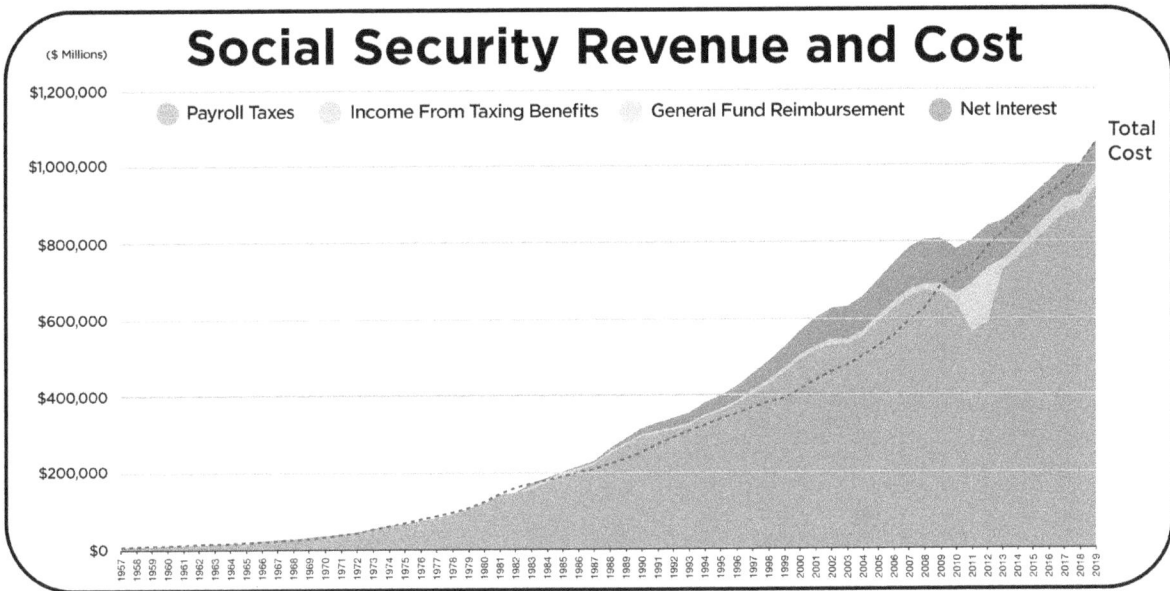

Source: https://en.wikipedia.org/wiki/Social_Security_%28United_States%29

What Pays for Social Security Benefits

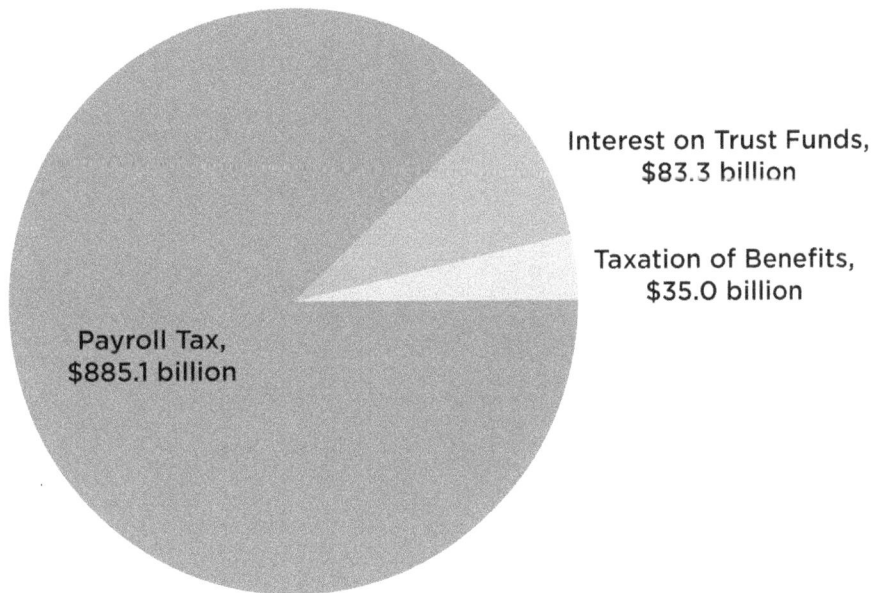

Interest on Trust Funds, $83.3 billion

Taxation of Benefits, $35.0 billion

Payroll Tax, $885.1 billion

Source: https://finance.yahoo.com/news/most-important-social-security-chart-110200809.html

QUESTIONS:

How confident are you that Social Security will be available when you retire? What are your reasons for thinking so?

....

....

....

....

....

What sources of income will you have to supplement Social Security if it is not enough to cover your expenses?

....

....

....

....

....

NOTES:

....

....

....

....

....

....

....

....

....

YOUR SOCIAL SECURITY BENEFITS

We all know that Social Security provides retirement benefits, but fewer people realize that it also covers disability and provides benefits for survivors after they die. These benefits can be especially crucial for younger families that experience the tragic loss of the family's primary wage earner.

Benefits are allocated based on "credits." Social Security work credits are earned based on your annual earnings that are subject to Social Security tax. The dollar amount required to earn one credit is set by the Social Security Administration and is adjusted over time to keep pace with wages. You can earn a maximum of four credits per year.

You can review your earnings record and current credit requirements by visiting the Social Security Administration website.

To receive retirement benefits, most workers need 40 credits to be considered "fully insured" by Social Security. In most cases, this requires working for at least ten years. In most cases, this requires that you work for at least ten years. In some cases, a person without enough work credits may be able to work part-time until they earn enough credits to be eligible.

It is also possible to qualify for retirement benefits based on a spouse's work history. Retirement benefits may be claimed as early as age 62 and as late as age 70, with higher monthly benefits paid for life if a later retirement date is chosen. This is a great strategy if you are in good health and do not need your retirement benefits earlier because you're still working or have other investment income you prefer to draw upon.

Although this workbook does not go into depth about the Social Security Disability Insurance (SSDI) and Supplemental Security Income (SSI) programs, I want to mention them briefly here. These programs provide assistance to adults and children who have disabilities and little income or other financial resources. The amount of the benefit depends on your age at the time you become disabled.

Before age 24, you can receive benefits if you earned six credits in the three years before your disability starts. From 24-31, you need credits for at least half the time between age 21 and the year of your disability. From 31-42, you need at least 20 credits. Starting at age 43, you need 20 credits plus one extra credit for each year you are older than 42. (For example, at 43, you need 21 credits, while at 44, you need 22 credits.) If the disability happens at age 62 or older, you need 40 credits to draw disability. If you qualify for these programs, you would probably be best served to engage a law firm specializing in disability benefits.

Social Security survivors benefits are paid to widows, widowers, and dependents of eligible workers. Survivors benefits do not always require you to have earned a full 40 credits. If you die, your surviving spouse may receive benefits if you have worked at least 1.5 years of the 3.25 years prior to your death. When someone passes away, the

Social Security Administration should be notified as soon as possible. In most cases, funeral homes will do so for the deceased if you provide their Social Security number. Alternatively, you can phone the SSA to report a death, but you cannot do so through the website.

Social Security benefits are available for your dependents if they have a parent who is disabled or retired and entitled to Social Security benefits, or if they have a parent who has died after working long enough to be eligible for benefits. In some cases, benefits are also available to stepchildren, grandchildren, step-grandchildren, or adopted children. Eligible dependents must meet one of the following criteria:

- Be younger than 18
- Be between 18 and 19 and a full-time high school student
- Be 18 or older with a disability that began before age 22

The intention of benefits for dependents is to stabilize family finances and make it possible for minors to complete high school. Children can receive up to 50% of their parents' retirement or disability benefits. In the case of a parent's death, children can get up to 75% of the parent's Social Security benefit. However, there is a ceiling to the amount Social Security will pay to a family, which totals 150% to 180% of the parent's full benefit amount. If the amount paid to all family members together goes over this limit, each child's benefit is reduced proportionately to get the family total down to the maximum allowed amount.

Social Security Benefits

Retirement Benefits
For workers 62 and older who have earned at least 40 credits

Disability Benefits
For adults 18 and older who are unable to work due to a physical or mental disability that is expected to last at least 12 months or result in death

Survivors Benefits
For the family members of deceased workers who qualified for Social Security

Source: https://www.fool.com/retirement/social-security/

How are Social Security benefits earned?

Work Credits

Your work history directly impacts your future benefits

40 Credits
needed for
Retirement and
Medicare benefits

$1,640 = 1 credit
in covered earnings

you can earn
a maximum of
4 credits
a year

Source: https://www.benzinga.com/money/social-security-vs-retirement-benefits

QUESTIONS:

Were you surprised to learn about any of the benefits available through Social Security?

....

....

....

....

....

Based on the description in this section, what benefits do you think you might qualify for?

....

....

....

....

....

NOTES:

HOW TO FILE FOR SOCIAL SECURITY

To receive Social Security benefits, you can retire as early as age 62 or as late as age 70. Spousal and survivors benefits can be claimed at other ages, but the first big decision you need to make is when you want your benefits to start. For each year you wait up to age 70, your monthly benefits will be higher for the rest of your life. This is a great choice for someone who has every reason to expect to live to their full life expectancy or beyond.

It is important to note that you don't *have* to start collecting Social Security by age 70. No one is going to force you to start drawing benefits. But if you wait past age 70, the benefits of waiting past full retirement age stop adding up. In other words, there is no additional benefit to waiting past age 70 to file.

Those with disabilities or chronic health issues who have reason to think they may not reach full life expectancy would be better advised to begin drawing benefits earlier. There is no "one size fits all" answer to this question. Rather, it depends on careful consideration of your individual circumstances.

You can file your application up to four months before the date you want your benefits to start. It's best to apply as soon as possible within this time frame since processing times can vary. The Social Security Administration may contact you for additional information, documents, or clarification, and there may be a delay between approval and receipt of your first payment. If you file your application late, you may be eligible to receive up to six months of retroactive benefits as a lump sum. However, choosing a retroactive start date can result in a lower ongoing monthly benefit, since it effectively moves your benefit start date earlier (source: https://PrepareforSocialSecurity.com/sources).

(It's helpful to note that the lump sum option potentially lowers your overall monthly benefit and therefore the total amount you receive over your lifetime, since it basically back-dates the application.)

There are four ways to file for Social Security benefits:

1. Complete a paper application, then mail it in or deliver it in person to a Social Security Administration office.

2. Complete an application with the help of a Social Security Administration employee in an SSA office. Make an appointment to avoid a long wait time.

3. Phone the SSA at 800-772-1213 to complete the application over the phone with a representative. Depending on the time you call, wait times may be substantial.

4. Open a "*my Social Security*" account on the SSA website and complete an online application.

Regardless of the method you choose, be aware that due to the complexities of the Social Security Program, inadequate training, and a high work volume, some SSA representatives may not be familiar with every rule or option that applies to your specific situation, particularly given the complexity of the Social Security system and the volume of cases they handle. It's important to do your own research or seek additional guidance when making decisions.

If you or the Social Security Administration makes a mistake in the application process, you can appeal to the SSA to change their decision. Once you receive a letter from the SSA with their decision on your application, you must make any appeals within 60 days, in writing. You can pursue your appeal through four levels to try to get the results you want:

1. A reconsideration by a different representative than the one who oversaw your application.
2. A hearing before an administrative law judge.
3. A review by the Social Security Administration's Appeals Council.
4. A review by the federal courts.

In addition to this formal appeals process, you can also hire a legal firm to help or reach out to your U.S. congressional representative for assistance in expediting the process.

You also have the option of withdrawing your application and starting again within the first 12 months of receiving benefits. However, the downside is that you will be required to repay all benefits received up to that point. In addition, the reapplication process will delay the start date of your newly calculated benefits.

In discussions about when to file for Social Security, the question inevitably comes up, "What happens if I don't file? Will I automatically start getting benefits?" The short answer is that the SSA is not going to start sending you money without you asking for it. Nobody is going to force you to file for Social Security at any point. Just keep in mind that your benefits will not increase if you wait past age 70 to file. In general, the longer you wait to file, the greater your benefits will be, but this advantage ceases once you turn 70 because the retirement credits stop accruing then.

However, there is one scenario in which your benefits will automatically begin at age 70. If you applied after you reached your full retirement age, then suspended your benefits until age 70, those benefits will automatically restart when you turn 70.

Website: https://www.ssa.gov/

National Phone Number: 1-800-772-1213

Email: https://secure.ssa.gov/emailus/

Postal mail:

Social Security Administration

Office of Public Inquiries and Communications Support

1100 West High Rise

6401 Security Blvd.

Baltimore, MD 21235

Find local office by ZIP code: https://secure.ssa.gov/ICON/main.jsp

OR

https://www.PrepareforSocialSecurity.com

QUESTIONS:

Which method of contacting the Social Security Administration will be more efficient for you?

....

....

....

....

....

If you have difficulty contacting them or working through the process, who is a trusted and knowledgeable family member or friend who can help you navigate the bureaucracy?

....

....

....

....

....

NOTES:

....

....

....

....

....

....

....

....

....

....

....

....

....

....

....

....

....

....

....

....

....

NOTES:

....

....

....

....

....

....

....

....

....

....

....

....

....

....

....

....

....

....

....

....

SECTION TWO:

PREPARE TO CHOOSE— MAKING YOUR BIG DECISION

In this section, we will guide you through some considerations and options for choosing when to file for Social Security.

DETERMINING YOUR BENEFIT AMOUNT

How big can you expect your monthly Social Security check to be? Your benefits are calculated based on the average of your 35 highest-earning years of work. Different formulas are applied depending on the year you were born. Those who have lower lifetime earnings will receive a higher percentage of their earnings in benefits.

What if you have less than 35 years of earnings? The Social Security Administration enters a "0" for each year without earnings, which reduces your monthly retirement benefit amount. Think back to middle school science class. If you failed to turn in an assignment and got a "0" score, what happened to your overall grade? The same principle applies here: if at all possible, you need to keep working until you have no zeros in any of the 35 years of your work record.

What if you choose to work for more than 35 years? This can actually be a great strategy if you are still in good health, have a job you like (or start a new career), and have some low-earning years on your work record you'd like to replace. If any of the years you work past your existing 35-year work record are at a higher income level, your lower-earning years will be automatically replaced with your higher-earning years. This will increase your overall benefit amount when you do start drawing Social Security.

The Social Security Administration has provided several ways to estimate your anticipated benefit amount long before you actually reach retirement age. Unfortunately, these different methods may produce very different results for reasons that are not always evident.

1. **Social Security Administration annual statement.** The SSA provides an annual Social Security statement showing what you have paid into the system and your estimated monthly benefit. Most people now access this statement online through a "my Social Security" account. However, it does not specify whether the amounts are in today's dollars or in the inflation-adjusted dollars of the year you will start drawing benefits. It also assumes no growth in Social Security's Average Wage Index, although this has increased nearly every year since 1952.

2. **Over-the-phone or in-person estimates at an SSA office.** Staff will provide a benefit estimate but, like the SSA annual statement, may not tell you what year's dollars the amount is quoted in or the assumptions the estimate makes about economic growth, inflation, or the Average Wage Index. If your quote is for an age over 65, they may reduce their quote by Medicare Part B premium payments and/or federal income tax withholding.

3. **Online benefits calculators.** Remarkably, the SSA provides four different online benefits calculators, but these vary in ease of use and accuracy. Don't be surprised if they generate four different numbers for you. You can find links to all these at https://PrepareforSocialSecurity.com/links.

   ○ The **Social Security Quick Calculator** shows results both in today's dollars and in future dollars (adjusted for cost of living).

   ○ The **Online Benefits Calculator** requires a bit more work. You have to input your earnings for every year you've worked.

   ○ The **Social Security Detailed Calculator** requires even more work. You have to download software to your computer and enter your year-by-year earnings history. On the plus side, it uses the most recent Cost of Living Adjustment to calculate your benefits.

   ○ The **Retirement Estimator** requires you to provide identifying information, including your Social Security number, and finds your actual earnings to produce a benefit estimate.

Social Security benefits calculators should be used as a rough guide. Those that assume zero inflation and wage growth generate lower benefit estimates, especially for younger workers. This might help incentivize younger workers to set aside more for retirement to supplement Social Security.

They can also overestimate your future benefits by assuming that you will continue to earn what you currently do all the way to full retirement age. In reality, if you move to lower-paying or part-time work *before* retirement, your benefit amount will likely be reduced. Why is this? Remember that your benefits are based on your 35 highest-earning years. If, in your last few years before retirement, your income declines, it may lower your average income for those 35 years from what it would have been had you continued working full-time at a high-paying job. Note that working a part-time job *after* retirement has no negative impact on your benefits, unless you exceed the annual earnings limit set by the SSA.

Hypothetical Historical Earnings of a Sample Worker

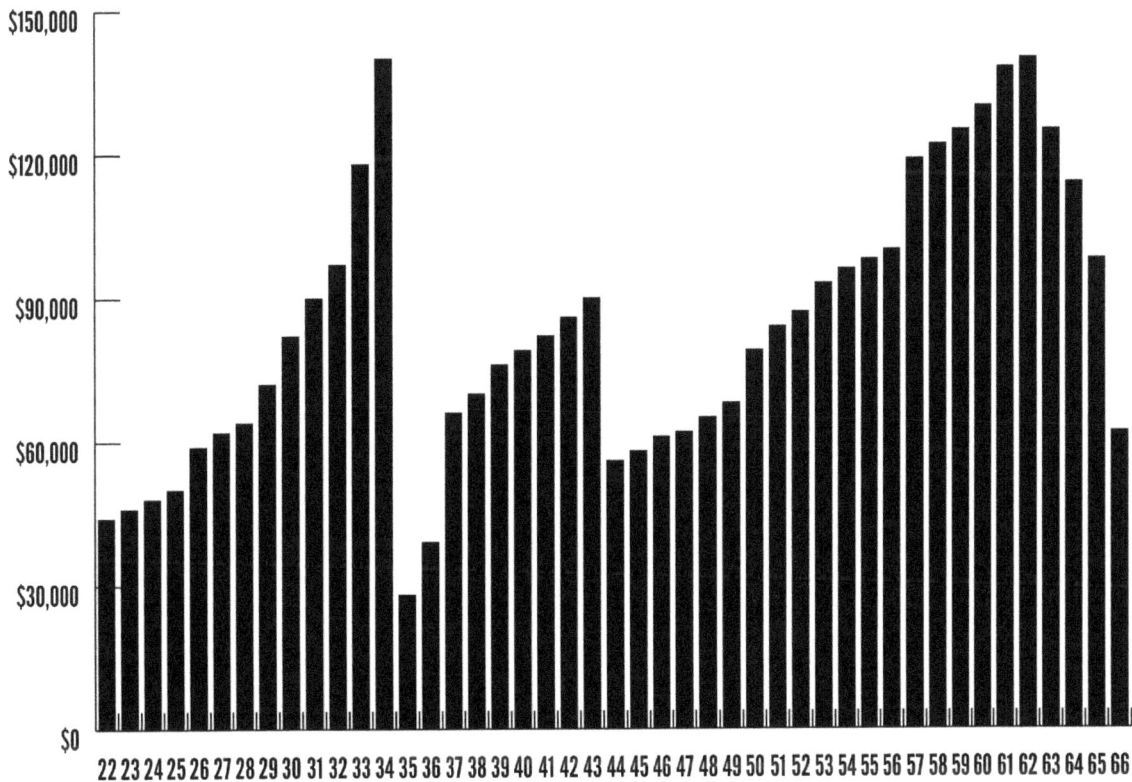

Source: https://www.kitces.com/blog/social-security-and-working-how-adding-to-social-security-work-history-can-increase-retirement-benefit/

QUESTIONS:

After trying two or three benefits calculators, are you getting similar results? If not, why do you think that might be?

....

....

....

....

....

If you have worked a bit less than 35 years, how feasible would it be for you to continue working until you have reached that point, knowing that it could substantially raise your retirement benefits?

....

....

....

....

....

NOTES:

....

....

....

....

....

....

....

....

....

....

....

....

....

....

....

....

....

....

....

....

....

....

DECIDING WHEN TO CLAIM YOUR BENEFITS

As you near retirement age, perhaps the single most important decision you will make about Social Security is when to claim your benefits. There is no "one size fits all" answer to this question. Some people will profit most by retiring as early as possible. Others would come out better financially in the end by waiting.

If you're married, you and your spouse might want to retire at different ages to maximize your income during retirement. You have to decide what is best for you based on a number of different factors, not all of which are purely financial.

Social Security rules allow you to start receiving benefits as early as age 62 or as late as age 70. The longer you wait, the higher your monthly benefit check will be. Drawing Social Security too early is one of the most common and costly mistakes people make in this process.

Claiming benefits at age 62 can permanently reduce your monthly benefit by roughly 25% to 30%, depending on your Full Retirement Age, and this can add up to thousands of dollars lost per year. If, on the other hand, you wait until age 70 to claim benefits, you can receive up to an additional 24% in your monthly benefit due to delayed retirement credits. And so, you will have thousands of dollars more per year for a lifetime.

Some people argue it's better to take retirement early because that will give you more benefit checks over your lifetime than if you wait. It doesn't matter how many checks you get, though–what matters is the total those checks add up to. Taking early benefits makes each check smaller than it otherwise would have been. Waiting until age 70 results in fewer checks but a much higher monthly benefit. In the end, people who live a full projected lifespan will get the greatest benefit from waiting until the maximum allowable age.

For some people, it can make sense to claim benefits earlier, such as in situations where they have dependents to care for, with no other sources of retirement income to live on. Another reason to claim early may be a family health history of chronic illness and shorter-than-average lifespans.

The Social Security Administration provides a convenient Life Actuarial Table, which you can access via https://PrepareforSocialSecurity.com/links. Alternatively, they also provide a Life Expectancy Calculator, which you can access via the Links page as well. When you enter your sex and date of birth, the system will generate a chart indicating the average number of additional years you can expect to live, on average, after reaching a specific age.

Remember, this is not a crystal ball. No one can predict with certainty the year you will pass away. When making a realistic projection of your life expectancy, you should consider several factors, such as how long people tend to live in your family; how healthy your own lifestyle is; what health conditions you already have; the amount of stress, anger, or worry in your life and how you are managing it; and whether you have healthy relationships or live a solitary life.

Life Expectancy (Years)

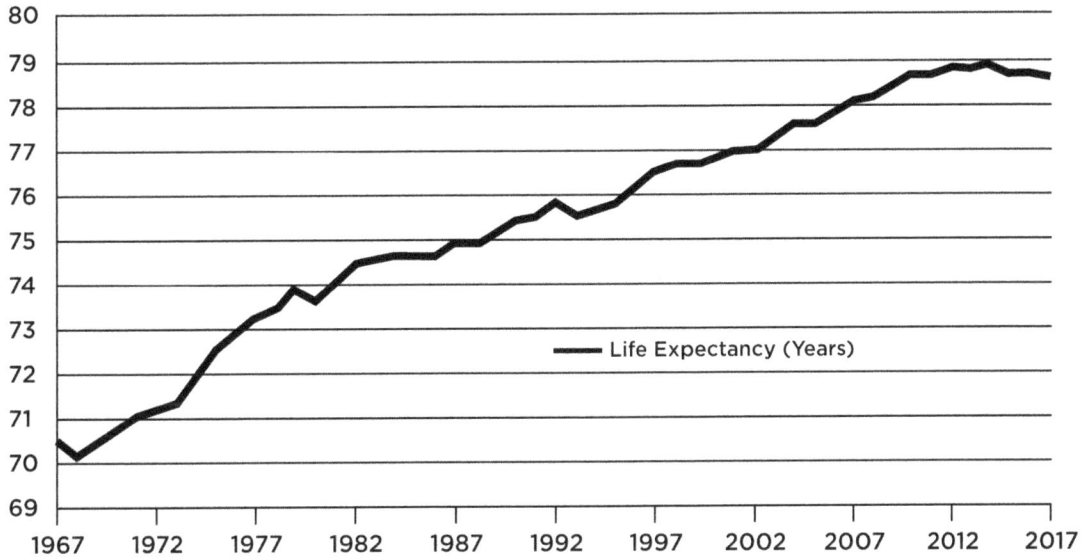

Source: https://pulmonarychronicles.com/index.php/pulmonarychronicles/article/view/529/1161

QUESTIONS:

Considering your life situation, are you leaning toward claiming benefits early, at full retirement age, or later?

....

....

....

....

....

Based on the Social Security Administration tools and your family history, what do you think is a reasonable estimate of your life expectancy?

....

....

....

....

NOTES:

SHOULD YOU USE THE BREAK-EVEN STRATEGY?

One approach to determining when you should retire is your "break-even" age. This is the age at which the dollar value of claiming benefits later equals the value of taking them early. It's hard to calculate this number exactly because of annual cost-of-living increases and income changes for people who are still working. However, it's possible to get a ballpark idea using a benefits calculator such as the one found on your Social Security account.

Be aware that many Social Security experts tell people not to use the break-even strategy. It can cost you a lot of money if you end up living longer than expected (although it's a great thing to live longer than expected!). Deciding the best age to retire is not a precise science. You should consider your health and other financial resources before making a decision.

To help illustrate the "break-even" age, let's consider the following scenario.

★ ★ ★ ★ ★

Let's imagine two coworkers, James and Naomi, who share the same Full Retirement Age under Social Security rules. Let's imagine that if they waited until their FRA to retire, they would each begin receiving $1,000 a month.

James decides to retire at age 62. As a result, his benefits are permanently reduced for early claiming, giving him a lower monthly Social Security check. In his first year of retirement, he brings in $8,400. By the time five years have passed, and he reaches FRA, he has already brought in $42,000, and Naomi has received *nothing!* Sorry, Naomi.

But... when Naomi retires in 2027 at age 67, she begins drawing $1,000 a month. She's getting $300 a month more than James now, which adds up to $3,600 more than him by the end of the year. How many years of this will it take her to catch up to him and his $42,000 head start? Divide $42,000 by $3,600, and you get 11 years and eight months. So at age 78 and eight months, the total benefits James and Naomi have received would be equal: this is their break-even age. After this point, Naomi will continue to pull ahead. If they both live another ten years, she will be $36,000 ahead of James.

Is there anything we overlooked? Oh yes, we forgot about Wanda over there in the next cubicle. She was also born in 1960. She decides to work past FRA and wait until age 70, the maximum, to retire. When she does, her benefits are increased due to delayed retirement credits, resulting in a higher monthly benefit than at Full Retirement Age.

James, by this point, is $67,200 ahead of her; Naomi retired just three years earlier and is only $10,800 ahead of her. But Wanda makes $540 a month ($6,480 a year) more than James. It takes her about ten years and four months to break even with him. But she makes $240 a month ($2,880 a year) more than Naomi. It takes her three years and nine months to break even with her.

Let's say she goes on to live to be 88. After these break-even points, in her remaining retirement years, she will receive about $49,442 more than James (88 - 80.37 = 7.63 years x $6,480) and about $41,040 more than Naomi (88 - 73.75 = 14.25 years x $2,880).

★　★　★　★　★

Here are some steps to figuring out your break-even points using the tools provided at www.ssa.gov/estimator:

- Find out your full retirement age.

- Figure out your full retirement benefit at that age.

- Determine your benefit at age 62.

- Determine how much you would receive in the 48 months between age 62 and your full retirement age if you start drawing your benefits at age 62.

- Figure out how many months you would have to live beyond 66 to break even.

If you are deciding between retiring at 62 rather than waiting until full retirement at 67, the break-even age is usually around 77 or 78. If you die earlier than that age, a break-even approach would say that taking the earlier retirement option would be beneficial. If you live longer than the break-even point, it would be better to wait until full retirement age to receive benefits.

If you are deciding between retiring at 67 or delaying retirement until 70, the break-even age is usually a few months after your 82nd birthday. If you die earlier than 82, the break-even approach would favor starting your benefits at 67. On the other hand, if you live past that break-even point, it would be better for you to have waited until age 70 to retire.

There are some important caveats. The break-even strategy can be misleading. It is not recommended by all advisors, certainly not in all situations. Some examples of problems with this strategy are (source: https://PrepareforSocialSecurity.com/sources):

- If you include cost-of-living increases in Social Security in a break-even analysis, it can make it appear more beneficial than it really is to delay filing. Moreover, while COLA (cost-of-living adjustment) increases average about 2.6%, it is not guaranteed. In some years there is no COLA increase.

- The break-even strategy does not consider how much more money you could have earned had you taken Social Security earlier and invested the money in more profitable financial instruments. On the other hand, each year you wait to take benefits between your full retirement age and age 70, your benefits increase by 8%. This increase may not be as large as what you may earn in an excellent stock market year—but it also comes with zero financial risk.

- A break-even approach might not make as much sense for a married couple as for an individual, especially in situations where your spouse may outlive you while drawing benefits based on your earnings record. If you accept lower monthly benefits, your spouse's benefits will be reduced as well. The life expectancy and financial needs of both spouses should be taken into account before making a decision.

It can be tempting to use the break-even point as a shortcut to give you the precise, optimal age you should claim benefits to get the best financial advantage. It doesn't work that way. Your situation, and that of your spouse, still require careful evaluation of a range of factors beyond those you type into a break-even calculator. Nonetheless, this tool can be one piece of the puzzle worthy of your consideration.

Standard Social Security Breakeven Analysis

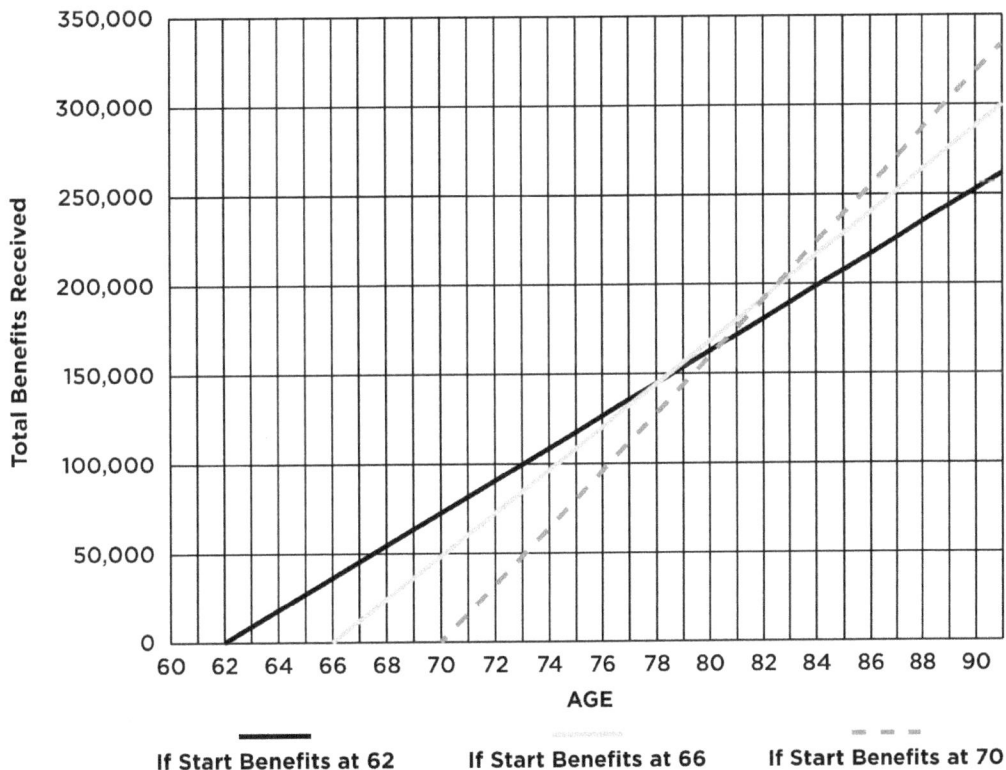

Source: https://www.fool.com/investing/2016/06/19/if-youre-thinking-about-delaying-social-security-u.aspx

QUESTIONS:

What may be some advantages of the break-even strategy in your situation?

....

....

....

....

....

What may be some disadvantages of the break-even strategy in your situation?

....

....

....

....

....

NOTES:

....

....

....

....

....

....

....

....

....

....

....

....

....

....

....

....

....

....

....

....

....

THE DOUBLE-WHAMMY EFFECT

The "double-whammy effect" refers to the fact that some Social Security benefits are subject to taxation. This was a decision made by Congress in 1983 to prevent the Social Security Trust Fund from running out of money.

Many retirees find this tax galling because it feels like paying taxes twice on the same income—once when it was earned at work, and again when the benefits are received. It's worth noting that many retirees receive much more in benefits than the amount they contributed to the system over the years, but that doesn't make the tax any more palatable for those who are subject to it.

Moreover, the thresholds for taxation have never been adjusted for inflation. So as benefits increase over the years, a larger number of people are subject to the tax. In effect, this allows the government to tax more retirees and receive more revenue from each retiree without having to make the politically unpopular decision to vote to raise taxes on retirement.

For better or worse, here's how it works. The tax applies only after a retiree's income exceeds a threshold amount. It generally affects those with moderate or higher incomes. As of this writing, some states also tax a portion of Social Security benefits. State tax rules change over time, so it's important to check current state-specific guidance before assuming your benefits will or will not be taxed (source: https://PrepareforSocialSecurity.com/sources).

At tax time, you have to add together your adjusted gross income, any municipal bond interest, and one half of your Social Security benefits for the year. If this number is higher than $25,000 for an individual or $32,000 for a couple filing jointly, then up to 50% of your Social Security benefit must be added to your taxable income. If your base amount is more than $34,000 for an individual or $44,000 for a couple, you may be taxed on as much as 85% of your Social Security benefits. In either case, the base amount is $0 for people married but filing separately. They will have to pay tax on at least 50% of their benefits.

What does this mean for your decision about when to draw Social Security? It's mainly a concern for those who have other sources of retirement income, such as a traditional IRA or 401(k). One hundred percent of withdrawals from those investments are taxable, whereas only 50-85% of Social Security income is taxable. If you prefer to reduce your tax burden, you might want to consider drawing Social Security earlier rather than beginning to tap those types of investments. However, note that Roth IRA withdrawals are not taxable as they are funded with after-tax money.

QUESTIONS:

Does your state tax Social Security benefits?

....

....

....

....

....

....

Will the amount of taxation be significant enough to affect your decision of what state to retire in?

....

....

....

....

....

....

NOTES:

SURVIVORS BENEFITS

When a worker dies, their spouse, child, or parent may be eligible to apply for Social Security benefits based on their work record, if the deceased person worked long enough to qualify for benefits.

Workers can earn up to four Social Security credits each year. These are based on total wages and self-employment income for the year. The amount of earnings it takes to earn a credit can change each year. Consult the "Social Security Credits" page on the SSA website for the current year's income requirements. (You can find it via our Links page at https://PrepareforSocialSecurity.com/links.)

The younger the worker is, the fewer credits they have earned, reducing the amount available for survivors benefits. However, survivors may get benefits even if the worker has credit for only 1.5 years of work (6 credits) in the three years prior to their death. This is especially important for very young widows or widowers who may have thought of Social Security as a benefit only available near retirement age.

When a member of the family dies, the SSA should be notified as soon as possible to avoid any delays in receiving survivors benefits. Funeral homes will typically notify the SSA for the family if they have been provided with the deceased person's Social Security number. Note that you cannot notify the SSA of a death or apply for survivors benefits online. Instead, you can call the SSA or visit a local SSA office to complete the report and application. If the deceased person was already drawing Social Security benefits, the benefit payment for the month of death and any subsequent months must be returned.

The SSA will provide a one-time lump sum death payment of $255 to the surviving spouse, or, if the spouse has also passed away, the payment will be made to a child who is eligible for survivors benefits in the month of the worker's death. To receive this lump sum, the beneficiary must have already been receiving benefits on the worker's record or must become eligible for benefits upon the worker's death. If they are not yet eligible to receive Social Security benefits, they may still apply for this death payment within two years of their loved one's passing.

A widow or widower may receive benefits based on the deceased's earnings history if the survivor is 60 years old or more (50 or older if they have become disabled within seven years of the spouse's death), or at any age if they are not remarried and are the caregiver to the deceased person's child who is under 16 or has a disability. If the survivor remarries after age 60 (age 50 if they have a disability), the remarriage will not affect eligibility for survivors benefits from the prior marriage. If they wish, the survivor may switch to their own retirement benefit as early as age 62. If they are eligible for both survivors benefits and retirement benefits, they can choose to apply for one and switch to the other, higher benefit later.

A person who became eligible for retirement benefits less than 12 months before their spouse's death has the option to withdraw their retirement application and apply for survivors benefits only, then apply for retirement benefits later when they are higher. Those who are already receiving retirement benefits at the time their spouse passes away can only apply for survivors benefits if the retirement benefit is less than the amount of survivors benefits. Applying for survivors benefits cannot be done online but may be done by phone or by appointment at a Social Security office.

A surviving divorced spouse can receive benefits just like a widow or widower as long as the marriage lasted ten years or longer. These benefits will not reduce the benefit amount for other survivors drawing benefits from the worker's earnings history, and they will not count against the family maximum that can be drawn based on that record. Even if the divorced spouse remarries, they will still be eligible for survivors benefits as long as they were at least 60 years old at the time of remarriage (50 if they have a disability).

Some special rules apply if the divorced spouse is caring for the former spouse's natural or legally adopted child who is under age 16 or has a disability. If the child is receiving benefits on the record of the former spouse, the surviving divorced spouse does not have to meet the length-of-marriage rule. Moreover, if you are in this circumstance of caring for your divorced spouse's child, your benefit *does* affect the amount of benefits available to others on the worker's record.

Children may receive Social Security benefits if they are unmarried. They must be younger than 18, up to 19 if they are a full-time elementary or high school student, or if they are older than 18 but have a disability that began before age 22. Stepchildren, grandchildren, step-grandchildren, and adopted children may also be eligible under certain circumstances.

If the parents of the deceased person depended on them for at least half of their support and are 62 or older, they may also be eligible for benefits. To receive benefits, the parents' own retirement benefits must not be higher than the benefit available on their child's work record. Moreover, the couple must not have married *after* the child's death, although there are some exceptions. Benefits are also available for stepparents or adoptive parents if they became parents before the child reached age 16.

The amount various survivors may receive is based on the earnings record of the person who died, the relationship of the survivor to the worker, their disability status, and the age at which they apply for survivors benefits. The chart below outlines what survivors benefits may look like for you:

Spouse or ex-spouse, full retirement age or older	100% of deceased worker's benefit amount
Spouse or ex-spouse, age 60	71.5% to 99%
Spouse or ex-spouse with disability, aged 50-59	71.5%
Spouse or ex-spouse, any age, caring for a child under 16	75%
Child, under 18, or 19 if still in school or who has a disability	75%
One dependent parent, 62 or older	82.5%
Two dependent parents, 62 or older	75% each

Deceased **DID NOT** File for Benefits	Died BEFORE Full Retirement Age	Deceased's full retirement age benefit (adjusted for survivor's filing age)
	Died AFTER Full Retirement Age	Deceased's benefit if they would have filed on the day of death (adjusted for survivor's filing age)
Deceased **DID** File for Benefits	Filed **ON or AFTER** Full Retirement Age	Benefit amount deceased was receiving at death (adjusted for survivor's filing age)
	Filed **BEFORE** Full Retirement Age	Maximum Benefit: Actual benefit of the deceased *or* 82.5% of the deceased's FRA benefit (adjusted for survivor's filing age)

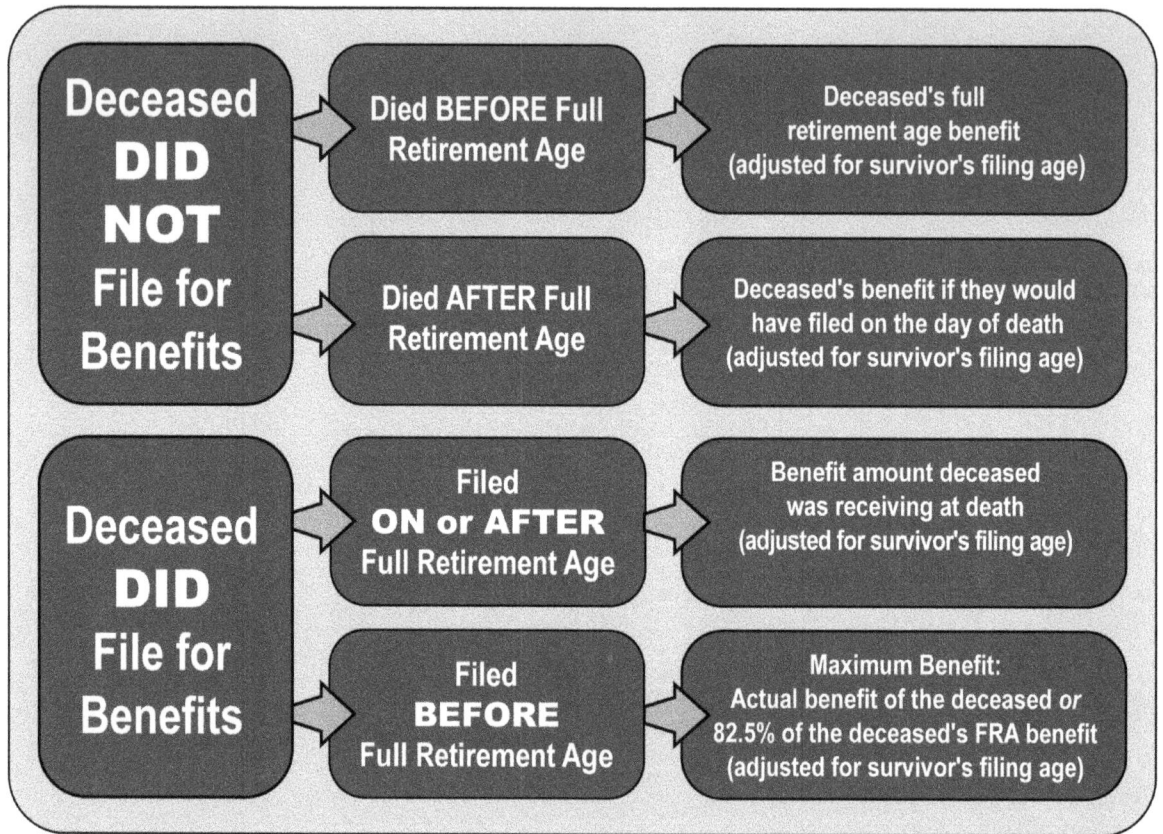

Source: https://www.socialsecurityintelligence.com/social-security-survivor-benefits-and-death/social-security-survivors-benefit-flow-chart/

QUESTIONS:

Could you be eligible for survivors benefits from a spouse or ex-spouse?

....

....

....

....

How can you make sure loved ones who might qualify for survivors benefits if you pass away are aware of this and what they need to do?

....

....

....

....

....

NOTES:

....

....

....

....

....

....

....

....

....

....

....

....

....

....

....

....

....

....

....

....

....

SOCIAL SECURITY EXEMPTIONS

Some jobs are not subject to Social Security taxes, but if you take advantage of one of these exemptions, you generally will not be eligible to receive Social Security retirement, disability, or survivor benefits based on that work.

Religious exemptions. You may claim a religious exemption from Social Security taxes if you are a member of a recognized religious group that is opposed to accepting Social Security benefits, including retirement and death or disability benefits. The group must have existed as of the end of 1950 and provided its members with a reasonable standard of living since then.

This is not an automatic exemption; you must claim it by filing Form 4029. If you have ever been eligible for Social Security benefits, the exemption is unavailable whether or not you actually received the benefit.

International exemptions. People who are not United States citizens or legal residents are considered nonresident aliens. Nonresident aliens who work in the United States pay Social Security tax on any income made in the country, even if they work for a foreign company. However, they are exempt if they work for a foreign government. Their families and domestic workers qualify for an exemption if they are also employed by a foreign government.

Foreign students and educators temporarily in the U.S. do not have to pay Social Security taxes. Depending on the type of visa the nonresident possesses, they may be eligible for the exemption.

Student exemptions. Students working for the school where they are enrolled who receive employment because of their enrollment may be exempt from paying Social Security taxes. This applies to money earned at the student's school, not wages earned from other employers.

Higher-earning exemption. There is a maximum income per year that the government may tax with Social Security. This means any income you earn above the maximum for the year is exempt from Social Security tax. The maximum amount of earnings subject to Social Security tax is set annually by the Social Security Administration and can change from year to year.

QUESTIONS:

Do any of the exemptions in this section apply to you?

....

....

....

....

....

If so, what alternative plans will you make to fund your retirement, since you will not be eligible for Social Security benefits if you do not pay into the system?

....

....

....

....

....

NOTES:

DIFFERENT LIFE SITUATIONS

Some life situations will significantly impact your Social Security retirement strategy. Marriage and divorce, for example, open additional opportunities to maximize your family resources. Be aware that any age difference or difference in earnings between you and your spouse needs to be taken into account before you decide that a given strategy is right for your situation.

One popular approach is the "62/70 split." In this scenario, the spouse with lower earnings begins drawing Social Security at age 62, while the higher-earning spouse waits to file for benefits at age 70. This may help the family hedge their bets in terms of potential gains or losses due to life expectancy issues. Additionally, depending on how and when benefits are claimed, a spouse may be eligible for spousal benefits during the years the higher-earning spouse delays claiming their own retirement benefit.

Another strategy sometimes discussed is "File and Suspend." Under current Social Security rules, when a worker voluntarily suspends their retirement benefit, any spousal benefits payable on that worker's record are also suspended. This means a spouse cannot receive spousal benefits while the worker's benefit is suspended.

A worker who suspends benefits may later restart them, typically by age 70, to take advantage of delayed retirement credits. During a voluntary suspension, however, no spousal benefits are payable on that worker's record.

Still another consideration is that the timing and amount of Social Security benefits you draw may bump you into another tax bracket. Anywhere from 50-85% of Social Security income may be taxable if it causes your modified adjusted gross income to reach certain thresholds. If this is your situation, you or your spouse might decide to delay drawing benefits or cut back on your work to keep your income at a certain level so that you're not working simply to pay taxes and not enjoying the benefits of your labor.

Being single or married will not increase or decrease your personal retirement benefit because it is based on *your* earnings record. Each partner in a marriage collects their separate benefits based on their own work history. A spouse may receive spousal benefits based on their partner's work history, but this will not reduce the benefits the working partner receives themselves.

If a spouse passes away, the survivor becomes eligible for survivors benefits when they turn 60 (or 50 if the surviving spouse is disabled). If, however, they remarry before reaching that age, they will lose that benefit from the deceased spouse's work record. If the *remarriage* ends by death or divorce, however, they can once again claim survivors benefits from their previous spouse, who is deceased. But if they wait to get remarried until after 60 (or 50 if they are disabled), they will not lose their survivors benefit from the first spouse.

Be aware there is a maximum family benefit that limits how much Social Security a family can receive based on one retiree's work record. This limit is calculated by taking into account benefits for retirement, disability payments, spousal benefits, and children's benefits. It is generally equal to 150%-180% of the basic benefit rate. If the amount payable to family members exceeds this limit, the benefits will be reduced proportionately among all eligible family members. Benefits paid to a surviving divorced spouse based on disability or age will not count as part of this maximum amount.

The rules for divorced spouses are similar to those who are separated by death, with a key difference being that anyone receiving benefits based on the work history of an ex-spouse will lose those benefits if they remarry, regardless of age. If you become single again due to death or divorce, you can begin collecting benefits based on your ex-spouse's work history again.

When divorced spouses are both still living at the time of retirement, your ex-spouse can draw Social Security calculated from your work record, even if you have remarried. This does not reduce the amount of Social Security you or your current spouse are entitled to. For an ex-spouse to claim these benefits, the marriage must have lasted at least ten years, the person making the claim must be unmarried and at least 62 years old, and the benefit they would receive based on their own earnings history must be less than what they would receive based on yours.

As long as you have been divorced for at least two years, your ex-spouse can receive benefits based on your earnings record, even if you have not yet applied for retirement benefits but can qualify for them. The SSA will pay the ex-spouse their own benefit and add to it an additional sum to bring it up to the full level of what they would have received from their partner if they had remained married.

An ex-spouse born before January 2, 1954 who has already reached full retirement age can, if they wish, elect to receive only the divorced spouse's benefit and wait until later to receive their own retirement benefit. However, for those born after this date, there is no longer the option to take only one benefit at full retirement age. Instead, if your ex-spouse files for one benefit, they will file for all retirement or spousal benefits.

ENTITLEMENT AND ELIGIBILITY RULES FOR SPOUSAL BENEFITS

Spousal Benefits		
Benefit Amount: 50% of worker's PIA		
Entitled		Eligible
Married	Divorced	Full benefit at Full Retirement Age (FRA)
Worker must have filed for his/her own benefit Must have been married for at least 1 year Must still be currently married	Worker must be at least age 62 Must have been married for at least 10 years, currently unmarried, and divorced for at least 2 years	Can start as early as age 62 (reduced by 8.33%/year, plus 5%/year beyond 3 years early) No delayed retirement credits past FRA

Source: https://www.kitces.com/blog/divorcee-social-security-spousal-benefits-rules-and-strategies/

QUESTIONS:

Do any of the special situations described in this section apply to you?

....

....

....

....

....

How will this affect your plans to claim Social Security benefits?

....

....

....

....

....

NOTES:

SHOULD YOU WORK WHILE DRAWING BENEFITS?

Many people erroneously believe you cannot work while drawing Social Security. This is a myth. In fact, when you do it, you and your family may actually increase your Social Security benefit. This is because every year your wages are reported to the SSA, they recalculate your benefits if your new year of work was one of your highest-earning 35 years.

The increase will be credited to you starting in January of the year after you earned these wages. Beginning with the month you reach full retirement age, your earnings will not reduce your benefits, no matter how much you earn.

Nevertheless, there are earnings limits for those who begin drawing benefits while they are younger than their full retirement age. Those who are younger than full retirement age and earn more than the annual earnings limit may have their benefits reduced at a rate of $1 deducted from their benefit payments for every $2 they earn above the annual limit, as set annually by the Social Security Administration. In the year you reach full retirement age, the SSA deducts $1 in benefits for every $3 earned above a higher earnings limit that applies only to the months before you reach full retirement age. Earnings are only counted up to the month before you reach full retirement age, not your earnings for the whole year. Deductions from your benefits are calculated based on wages, bonuses, commissions, and vacation pay but do not include pensions, annuities, investment income, interest income, veterans benefits, or other government or military retirement benefits.

To better understand your individual situation when it comes to working while drawing benefits, use the SSA's Earnings Test Calculator. You can also consult the publication "How Work Affects Your Benefits," which explains the rules related to working while drawing Social Security in more detail. Both of these resources are available at https://PrepareforSocialSecurity.com/links.

Here are some case studies related to working after drawing benefits:

- Marty retired and began drawing benefits, but he continued working in his flower shop. In the previous year, his gross wages were among the highest-earning 35 years of his working career. Because the SSA reviews the records of all Social Security beneficiaries who reported wages the previous year, Marty's benefits were recalculated, and he received an increased monthly benefit, payable retroactively to January of the year after he earned the money. If Marty's earnings were not higher than any of his 35 highest-earning years, then this would not decrease his monthly benefit amount.

- Seth decided to file for Social Security before reaching full retirement age and while continuing to work. Seth's income exceeded the annual earnings limit by $10,000. The SSA deducted $1 from his benefits for every $2 he earned above his limit. This means Seth's benefits were reduced for the year by $5,000. Of course, because he earned a total of $10,000 more than the limit, this means he still came out $5,000 ahead for the year. If he needs the money badly, it may be worth it to him to, in effect, receive only 50% of his earnings over the limit.

- Millie waited until she reached full retirement age to claim her benefits, and she decided to keep working in her home business as well. In the year that she reached FRA, the Social Security Administration looked at her earnings for the months of that year before her birthday. If she exceeded the earnings limit that applies in the year she reached full retirement age for the months before her birthday, her benefit would be reduced by $1 for every $3 over the limit she goes. So if she goes $3,000 over the limit (earning $54,960) during those months, her benefit amount will be reduced by $1,000.

Beginning with the month that Millie reached full retirement age, according to the rules, her earnings no longer reduced her benefits, no matter how much she earned. With this knowledge in mind, Millie decided to cut back on her work hours and just enjoy some vacation time with her family in the months leading up to her birthday to stay under the $51,960 limit. After her birthday, she began working extra hours in her business and pushed her income above $100,000 for the year. This did not reduce her Social Security benefits at all.

How does working in retirement affect benefits?

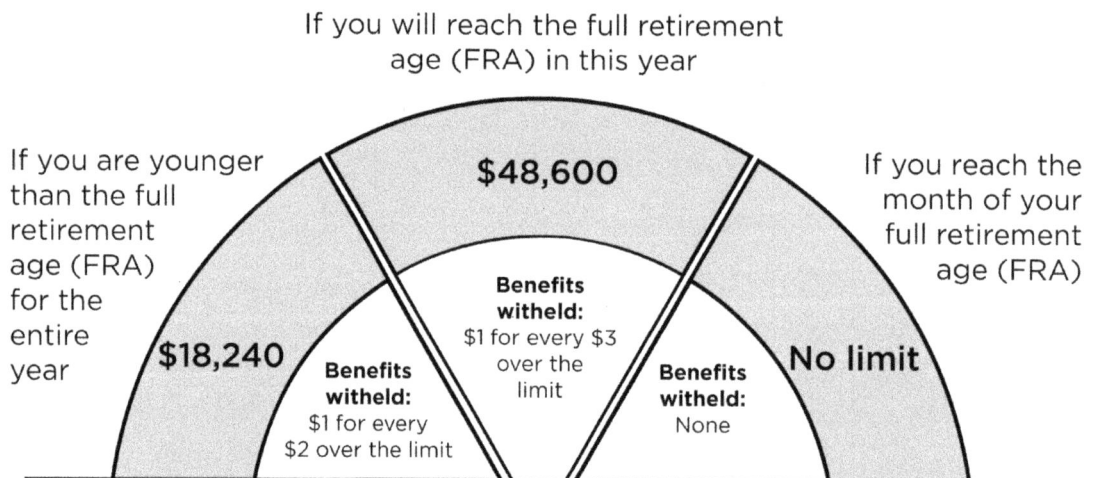

If you will reach the full retirement age (FRA) in this year

If you are younger than the full retirement age (FRA) for the entire year

$48,600

If you reach the month of your full retirement age (FRA)

$18,240

Benefits witheld:
$1 for every $2 over the limit

Benefits witheld:
$1 for every $3 over the limit

Benefits witheld:
None

No limit

Source: https://www.weingartenassociates.com/blog-01/social-security-benefits-while-working-how-are-your-benefits-affected

QUESTIONS:

Will you be able and willing to continue working after claiming Social Security?

....

....

....

....

....

How will working affect your benefits?

....

....

....

....

....

NOTES:

HOW TO READ YOUR SOCIAL SECURITY STATEMENT

You can easily see your Social Security statements by logging into your "*my Social Security*" account or creating one if you haven't already.

Your Social Security statement will contain several pieces of beneficial information:

- Retirement Benefits – whether or not you have enough credits to qualify for retirement benefits, as well as your full retirement age.

- Disability Benefits – how much you would receive per month if you became disabled right now.

- Survivors Benefits – how much various members of your family would receive in benefits if you were to die today.

- Personalized Monthly Retirement Benefit Estimates – showing your estimated benefit retiring each year (from 62 to 70 years old).

- Medicare – if you qualify for Medicare, and how to sign up.

- Earnings Record – how much of your earnings have been taxed for Social Security over your working lifetime.

- Earnings not covered by Social Security – a reminder that you may have some earnings, such as work for the government or a pension or retirement plan, that were not taxed for Social Security.

- A list of other important things to know about your Social Security benefits.

Your statement will also include a fact sheet based on your current age. You can also see the fact sheets on their own anytime by going to https://www.ssa.gov/myaccount/statement.html.

Your Estimated Benefits

*Retirement   You have earned enough credits to qualify for benefits. At your current earnings rate, if you continue working until...

your full retirement age (67 years), your payment would be about...$ 1,619 a month

age 70, your payment would be about ....$ 2,023 a month

age 62, your payment would be about ....$ 1,113 a month

*Disability   You have earned enough credits to qualify for benefits. If you became disabled right now,

your payment would be about..$ 1,441 a month

*Family   If you get retirement or disability benefits, your spouse and children also may qualify for benefits.

*Survivors   You have earned enough credits for your family to receive survivors benefits. If you die this year, certain members of your family may qualify for the following benefits:

Your child..$ 1,131 a month

Your spouse who is caring for your child..$ 1,131 a month

Your spouse, if benefits start at full retirement age..$ 1,508 a month

Total family benefits cannot be more than ....$ 2,778 a month

Your spouse or minor child may be eligible for a special one-time death benefit of $255.

Medicare   You have enough credits to qualify for Medicare at age 65. Even if you do not retire at age 65, be sure to contact Social Security three months before your 65th birthday to enroll in Medicare.

* Your estimated benefits are based on current law. Congress has made changes to the law in the past and can do so at any time. The law governing benefit amounts may change because, by 2033, the payroll taxes collected will be enough to pay only about 77 percent of scheduled benefits.

We based your benefit estimates on these facts:

Your date of birth (please verify your name on page 1 and this date of birth).................................   April 5, 1973

Your estimated taxable earnings per year after 2013 .... $44,833

Your Social Security number (only the last four digits are shown to help prevent identity theft).........   XXX-XX-1234

How Your Benefits Are Estimated

To qualify for benefits, you earn "credits" through your work — up to four each year. This year, for example, you earn one credit for each $1,160 of wages or self-employment income. When you've earned $4,640, you've earned your four credits for the year. Most people need 40 credits, earned over their working lifetime, to receive retirement benefits. For disability and survivors benefits, young people need fewer credits to be eligible.

We checked your records to see whether you have earned enough credits to qualify for benefits. If you haven't earned enough yet to qualify for any type of benefit, we can't give you a benefit estimate now. If you continue to work, we'll give you an estimate when you do qualify.

What we assumed — If you have enough work credits, we estimated your benefit amounts using your average earnings over your working lifetime. For 2013 and later (up to retirement age), we assumed you'll continue to work and make about the same as you did in 2011 or 2012. We also included credits we assumed you earned last year and this year.

Generally, the older you are and the closer you are to retirement, the more accurate the retirement estimates will be because they are based on a longer work history with fewer uncertainties such as earnings fluctuations and future law changes. We encourage you to use our online Retirement Estimator at *www.socialsecurity.gov/estimator* to obtain immediate and personalized benefit estimates.

We can't provide your actual benefit amount until you apply for benefits. **And that amount may differ from the estimates stated above because:**

(1) Your earnings may increase or decrease in the future.

(2) After you start receiving benefits, they will be adjusted for cost-of-living increases.

(3) Your estimated benefits are based on current law. **The law governing benefit amounts may change.**

(4) Your benefit amount may be affected by **military service, railroad employment or pensions earned through work on which you did not pay Social Security tax.** Visit *www.socialsecurity.gov* to learn more.

Windfall Elimination Provision (WEP) — In the future, if you receive a pension from employment in which you do not pay Social Security taxes, such as some federal, state or local government work, some nonprofit organizations or foreign employment, and you also qualify for your own Social Security retirement or disability benefit, your Social Security benefit may be reduced, but not eliminated, by WEP. The amount of the reduction, if any, depends on your earnings and number of years in jobs in which you paid Social Security taxes, and the year you are age 62 or become disabled. For more information, please see *Windfall Elimination Provision* (Publication No. 05-10045) at *www.socialsecurity.gov/WEP*.

Government Pension Offset (GPO) — If you receive a pension based on federal, state or local government work in which you did not pay Social Security taxes and you qualify, now or in the future, for Social Security benefits as a current or former spouse, widow or widower, you are likely to be affected by GPO. If GPO applies, your Social Security benefit will be reduced by an amount equal to two-thirds of your government pension, and could be reduced to zero. Even if your benefit is reduced to zero, you will be eligible for Medicare at age 65 on your spouse's record. To learn more, please see *Government Pension Offset* (Publication No. 05-10007) at *www.socialsecurity.gov/GPO*.

Your Earnings Record

Years You Worked	Your Taxed Social Security Earnings	Your Taxed Medicare Earnings
1989	1,489	1,489
1990	2,663	2,663
1991	4,483	4,483
1992	6,221	6,221
1993	7,491	7,491
1994	9,224	9,224
1995	11,897	11,897
1996	14,677	14,677
1997	17,434	17,434
1998	20,071	20,071
1999	22,827	22,827
2000	25,588	25,588
2001	27,576	27,576
2002	29,004	29,004
2003	30,772	30,772
2004	33,097	33,097
2005	35,102	35,102
2006	37,501	37,501
2007	39,927	39,927
2008	41,487	41,487
2009	41,446	41,446
2010	42,973	42,973
2011	44,833	44,833
2012		Not yet recorded

You and your family may be eligible for valuable benefits:

When you die, your family may be eligible to receive survivors benefits.

Social Security may help you if you become disabled— even at a young age.

A young person who has worked and paid Social Security taxes in as few as two years can be eligible for disability benefits.

Social Security credits you earn move with you from job to job throughout your career.

Total Social Security and Medicare taxes paid over your working career through the last year reported on the chart above:

Estimated taxes paid for Social Security:		Estimated taxes paid for Medicare:	
You paid:	$32,239	You paid:	$7,955
Your employers paid:	$33,994	Your employers paid:	$7,955

Note: In 2012, you paid 4.2 percent in Social Security taxes on your salary (up to $110,100) and 1.45 percent in Medicare taxes on your entire salary. Your employer paid 6.2 percent in Social Security taxes and 1.45 percent in Medicare taxes for you. If you are self-employed, you paid the combined employee and employer amount of 10.4 percent in Social Security taxes on your net earnings (up to $110,100) and 2.9 percent in Medicare taxes on your entire net earnings.

Help Us Keep Your Earnings Record Accurate

You, your employer and Social Security share responsibility for the accuracy of your earnings record. Since you began working, we recorded your reported earnings under your name and Social Security number. We have updated your record each time your employer (or you, if you're self-employed) reported your earnings.

Remember, it's your earnings, not the amount of taxes you paid or the number of credits you've earned, that determine your benefit amount. When we figure that amount, we base it on your average earnings over your lifetime. If our records are wrong, you may not receive all the benefits to which you're entitled.

Review this chart carefully using your own records to make sure our information is correct and that we've recorded each year you worked. You're the only person who can look at the earnings chart and know whether it is complete and correct.

Some or all of your earnings from **last year** may not be shown on your *Statement*. It could be that we still were

processing last year's earnings reports when your *Statement* was prepared. Your complete earnings for last year will be shown on next year's *Statement*. **Note:** If you worked for more than one employer during any year, or if you had both earnings and self-employment income, we combined your earnings for the year.

There's a limit on the amount of earnings on which you pay Social Security taxes each year. The limit increases yearly. Earnings above the limit will not appear on your earnings chart as Social Security earnings. (For Medicare taxes, the maximum earnings amount began rising in 1991. Since 1994, **all** of your earnings are taxed for Medicare.)

Call us right away at 1-800-772-1213 (7 a.m.–7 p.m. your local time) if any earnings for years **before last year** are shown incorrectly. Please have your W-2 or tax return for those years available. (If you live outside the U.S., follow the directions at the bottom of page 4.)

Source: https://www.ssa.gov/policy/docs/ssb/v74n2/v74n2p1.html

QUESTIONS:

What questions do you still have about how to read a Social Security statement?

....

....

....

....

....

How can you find answers to those questions?

....

....

....

....

....

NOTES:

....

....

....

....

....

....

....

....

....

....

....

....

....

....

....

....

....

....

....

....

....

STEPS TO CONSIDER WHEN MAKING YOUR BIG DECISION

Here are a few steps to consider when making your decision about applying for Social Security benefits:

- Review the rules for when you qualify for full benefits and know your options.

- Use various Social Security retirement calculators to get a general idea of what your benefit amount might be if you retire at different ages. The longer you wait to retire, the higher your monthly benefit will be.

- Estimate your life expectancy using the tool available on the SSA website along with your own evaluation of your and your family's health history and lifestyle habits.

- Review your income sources and expenses, including pensions and any other retirement savings instruments you hold. Look through your budget (or create one if you haven't already!) to see how much you actually need to live on.

- Consider whether you are able and willing to work, and what kinds of work may be open to you.

- Think about what your surviving spouse will need to live on if you pass away first. What is their estimated life expectancy? Will a health or disability issue require substantial resources?

- Be honest with yourself: could you wait just one more year to start your Social Security benefits? Based on what you have learned so far in this book, waiting one more year could have a notable effect on your benefits, particularly if that means you will reach full retirement age or even age 70.

SECTION THREE:

PREPARE TO FILE— DOING IT YOURSELF (DIY)

In this section, we will guide you through the process of filing for Social Security if you are going through the process on your own.

DECIDING WHETHER TO DIY

The first decision you need to make is whether to manage your Social Security decisions yourself, hire an advisor or consultant, or use free online tools and services. You can find a wealth of information at https://PrepareforSocialSecurity.com.

When making this decision, remember that you want to do everything in your power to claim the benefits that are rightfully yours. While you can certainly try to make it a go on your own, a professional can be a big help. A professional can help you sort through those options quickly to find the optimal ones for you.

But no matter which direction you go, you will file for Social Security and, in all likelihood, receive benefits. Depending on when you file, your benefit amount will be different, but it is determined by how long you work, how much you earn while you work, and the age at which you file.

Doing the research, making the decisions, and filing on your own saves you money in the short run. You don't have to pay any consultants' or advisors' fees, whether percentage-based, hourly, or one-time fees. All the control is yours. If your situation is not complicated and you take the time to do your research well, you can come out with similar results as if you hired a professional.

On the other hand, navigating Social Security on your own can mean losing out on money. Studies suggest that only a small percentage of retirees claim Social Security at an optimal time, with the remaining households potentially losing significant lifetime benefits—often totaling tens of thousands of dollars per household (Source: https://PrepareforSocialSecurity.com/sources).

If you don't know exactly what you're doing when you retire and start claiming benefits, you can miss out on a lot of money without knowing it. This loss could be far more significant than anything you would conceivably have to pay a professional to get it done right in the first place.

Hiring a consultant can also ease your workload. You will still need to provide a significant amount of information to your consultant and make the final decisions yourself. No one else can make your Social Security decisions for you. However, you can appoint a representative who will have eFolder access to your documents through the Social Security Administration and can keep track of critical communications regarding your benefits.

If an advisor is willing to offer any of these services for free, you should take full advantage. Why would anyone give you free service? They may be selling other financial planning tools, insurance policies, or retirement investment plans that are their primary source of income. You may need to listen to a sales pitch, but you are under no obligation to purchase any other plans or services that you can't afford or are just not right for you. Offering complimentary Social Security advice is a way for them to get potential customers in the door.

★ ★ ★ ★ ★

Pros of the DIY approach:

- You are the person most motivated to find the best solution for you.
- DIY saves you money from paying a professional.
- It keeps you empowered and in control.

Cons of the DIY approach:

- It can be a lot of work and stress to research Social Security options.
- You may make a mistake that can cost you a lot of money.
- A professional may be better equipped to communicate with the SSA and navigate appeals or corrections on your behalf.

★ ★ ★ ★ ★

QUESTIONS:

Does the idea of taking a "do it yourself" approach to filing for Social Security appeal to you? Why or why not?

....

....

....

....

....

Is it feasible for you to hire a professional, or ask a family member or friend to help if you run into difficulty?

....

....

....

....

....

NOTES:

FILING YOUR APPLICATION

There are three ways to complete the application. The easiest is to apply online, though you can also choose to phone or go to a Social Security office.

APPLYING ONLINE

- To start your application, go to the Social Security Administration website, navigate to the "Apply for Benefits" page, and read and agree to the Terms of Service. Click "Next."
- Review the "Getting Ready" section on the next page to ensure you have the information you need to apply.
- Select "Start a New Application."
- Answer the questions about who is filling out the application.
- You will be prompted to sign in to your Social Security account or to create one.
- Complete the application.

The SSA provides a few tips for completing this application. First, they note that for security reasons, it is best not to leave the application open without activity for an extended period of time. Additionally, if you get stuck on a question, you can move on to a different question and return at a later point. You can save your application and finish it later if you need. You can also access saved applications by going to "Return to a Saved Application" after you sign in. Finally, some answers (such as addresses) do not allow using periods, commas, or other special characters. If you get a message that your answer isn't valid, check this first since it is likely the culprit.

Once you have completed the application, the website will give you a chance to confirm your answers and make any necessary changes. It will ask if the answers are true to the best of your knowledge, and inform you that you can be held liable if you have provided false or misleading information in your application. After you have reviewed your information, you can click "submit now" to digitally sign your application. The website will then provide a confirmation number which you can use to check the status of your application.

If you want to complete your application at the local Social Security office, check your local office's number, location, and driving directions by navigating to the Prepare for Social Security website (https://PrepareforSocialSecurity.com) and entering your ZIP Code. You can also call 1-800-772-1213 to apply by phone during the SSA's published business hours.

To be ready for the application, you will need the following information and documents:

- Your date of birth, place of birth, and Social Security number.

- The name, Social Security number, and date of birth or age of your spouse(s), current or former. You should also know the dates and places of marriage and dates of divorce or death (if applicable).

- The names of any unmarried children under age 18, age 18-19 and in elementary or secondary school, or disabled before age 22.

- Your bank or other financial institution's Routing Transit Number and the account number.

- Your citizenship status.

- Whether you or someone on your behalf has ever filed for Social Security benefits, Medicare, or Supplemental Security Income.

- Whether you have used any other Social Security number.

- If you are applying for retirement benefits, the month you want your benefits to begin; and

- If you are within three months of age 65, whether you want to enroll in Medicare Part B (Medical Insurance).

- The name and address of your employer(s) for the current and previous year.

- How much money you earned in the current and previous years. Depending on when you file, you may also need to estimate your anticipated earnings for the following year.

- A copy of your Social Security statement or your earnings record. If you do not have a statement, you can view your Social Security statement online by creating an account and signing in. Even if you do not have a record of your earnings or are unsure if they are correct, you should fill out your application, and the SSA will help you review your earnings.

- The beginning and end dates of any active U.S. military service you had before 1968.

- Whether you became unable to work because of illnesses, injuries, or conditions at any time within the past 14 months. If "Yes," they will also ask the date you became unable to work.

- Whether you or your spouse have ever worked for the railroad industry.

- Whether you have earned Social Security credits under another country's Social Security system; and

- Whether you qualified for or expect to receive a pension or annuity based on your own employment with the federal government of the United States or one of its states or local subdivisions.

Additional documents you may need:

- Your original birth certificate or other proof of birth.
- Proof of U.S. citizenship or lawful alien status if you were not born in the United States.
- A copy of your U.S. military service paper(s), e.g., DD-214 Certificate of Release or Discharge from Active Duty, and
- A copy of your W-2 form(s) and/or self-employment tax return for last year.

The SSA will accept copies of W-2 forms, self-employment tax returns, or medical documents but must see the original of most other documents, including your birth certificate. These will be returned to you.

When mailing documents to the SSA, be sure to include your Social Security number on a separate sheet of paper so that they will be matched to the correct file. If you have foreign birth records or documents from the Department of Homeland Security, do not mail them because they are extremely difficult to replace. Instead, bring them to your local Social Security office for examination.

You should keep careful records so you can confirm your income from every year you worked, preferably with tax information as well. This ensures you are getting your proper benefit amount. That way, you can double-check the benefit amount by logging in to your account and confirming that it's correct.

QUESTIONS:

Which means of filing for Social Security would work best for you?

....

....

....

....

....

Are you missing any of the necessary documents to file for Social Security? How can you obtain replacements for them?

....

....

....

....

....

NOTES:

....

....

....

....

....

....

....

....

....

....

....

....

....

....

....

....

....

....

....

....

DETERMINING YOUR BENEFIT AMOUNT

Benefits calculators can be incredibly helpful in giving you information to help you make good decisions related to Social Security. However, it is generally best not to rely on only one benefits calculator when making your decision about when to retire and start claiming benefits. Even excellent tools can have occasional bugs. Also, be aware that Social Security benefits may increase over time through cost-of-living adjustments, though these adjustments are not guaranteed every year. (You can find links to all the resources mentioned here by visiting https://PrepareforSocialSecurity.com/links.)

One excellent calculator is the Retirement Estimator from the SSA itself. This calculator uses your actual earnings record through your *"my Social Security"* account to give your estimate. This tool does not recommend the best age to start benefits, but it does show your estimated benefits if you start payments at age 62, full retirement age, and age 70. Additionally, you can only use this tool if you have enough Social Security credits (40 credits).

If you don't have and don't want to have a *"my Social Security"* account yet, you can use the "Online Benefits Calculator" from the SSA. However, you must put in all your earnings information every time you use it to get an accurate estimate. Because of this, they recommend using the *"my Social Security"* account since it is easier and faster.

The fastest SSA calculator is the Quick Calculator, which uses very little data and, as such, is not necessarily accurate. It "makes an initial assumption about your past earnings," which you will have an opportunity to change to make it more accurate.

The SSA also provides a Retirement Age Calculator, which shows your full retirement age based on your year of birth, as well as an Early or Late Retirement Calculator. This one will show the estimated impact on your benefits if you retire earlier or later than your full retirement age.

All SSA calculators are available on their "Benefits Calculators" page. If you plan to have additional income during retirement, the Retirement Earnings Test Calculator from the SSA can estimate how much of your benefit might be temporarily withheld due to the earnings test.

You can also use any number of third-party retirement calculators, which again only provide estimates. You can find a list of these on our Links page at https://PrepareforSocialSecurity.com/links.

QUESTIONS:

What were the results when you tried two or more of the referenced benefit calculators? Were you surprised?

....

....

....

....

....

If your projected benefits are less than you need for your living expenses in retirement, what are some possibilities for you to supplement your income?

....

....

....

....

....

NOTES:

....

....

....

....

....

....

....

....

....

....

....

....

....

....

....

....

....

....

....

....

DO YOU NEED TO PAY TAXES?

As we discussed in Section Two, the "double-whammy effect" refers to the fact that some Social Security benefits are subject to taxation. The tax is only applied after your income exceeds a threshold amount. It generally affects those with moderate or higher incomes. As of this writing, some states tax a portion of Social Security benefits. State rules change periodically, so be sure to verify current treatment based on your state of residence (source: https://PrepareforSocialSecurity.com/sources).

For a detailed discussion of how Social Security taxes work, please revisit Section Two. For now, the most important thing to remember is that Social Security taxes are mainly a concern for those who have other sources of retirement income, such as a traditional IRA or 401(k). One hundred percent of withdrawals from those investments is taxable, whereas only 50-85% of Social Security income is taxable. If you prefer to reduce your tax burden, you might want to consider drawing Social Security earlier rather than beginning to tap those types of investments. However, note that Roth IRA withdrawals are not taxable as they are funded with after-tax money. For the most up-to-date information on Social Security taxes, income limits, and many other related topics, visit https://PrepareforSocialSecurity.com.

QUESTIONS:

Does your state tax Social Security benefits?

....

....

....

....

....

Will the amount of taxation be significant enough to affect your decision of what state to retire in?

....

....

....

....

....

NOTES:

APPEALING A DECISION

Many of the decisions made by the SSA can be appealed if you disagree with them. In their language, the initial decisions they make are called "initial determinations." These constitute the SSA's findings on legal issues, the amount of your benefit payment, and issues related to overpayments, and they can be appealed.

Whenever the SSA makes an initial determination, they will send you a notice. Then you have 60 days to appeal that determination in writing. The notice will tell you both how to appeal and whether you are entitled to continued benefits while you appeal.

Be forewarned that when you appeal an SSA decision, they will reexamine your entire case, even those parts that were favorable to you. This means there is a chance that some of your benefits may be reduced through the appeals process if they realize they made a mistake that turned out to be favorable to you.

There are four levels, or steps, in the appeals process. (Visit https://PrepareforSocialSecurity.com/links for links to SSA pages that go into more detail about each of these levels.)

The first is "Reconsideration." If you don't agree with the SSA's initial determination, you may request reconsideration. The quickest way to do this is to go to the "Appeal a Decision" page and choose the right reconsideration, whether medical or non-medical. You can also submit a form by mail or fax. This will be "a complete review of your claim by someone who did not take part in the first determination. They will look at all the evidence used in the first determination, plus any new evidence that they obtain or that you submit."

The second level of appeal, if you don't agree with the reconsideration determination, is a "Hearing by Administrative Law Judge." There is an online request form where you will select whether it is medical or non-medical. While you may ask the judge to make a decision based on the evidence in your file, you are much more likely to be successful if you or your representative appear before the judge for the hearing. You can request that your hearing take place in person, by video teleconference, or by telephone, but the SSA will determine the manner of your court appearance in the end. The judge may ask medical and vocational experts to testify at the hearing.

The third level of appeal, if you don't agree with the judge's decision, is an Appeals Council review. You can submit a written appeal or fill out an online form. Like the others, this must be submitted within 60 days after the previous decision. You can submit or inform the council about new evidence. The Appeals Council will consider an appeal based on additional evidence if it is new and relevant, and if it is reasonable to think it would affect the final decision. From there, they decide whether or not to grant your request for review. They may deny or dismiss the request if they concluded the decision conforms to Social Security law and regulations. They may also decide to issue a new decision or send it to an administrative law judge for a decision.

Finally, the fourth and final level of appeal, if all else fails, is the Federal Court review. If you disagree with the action of the Appeals Council, you may file a civil action in the U.S. District Court in your area. Note that the SSA will not help you file this, and you will not be able to file online. You will likely need a lawyer or other legal counsel to take this step.

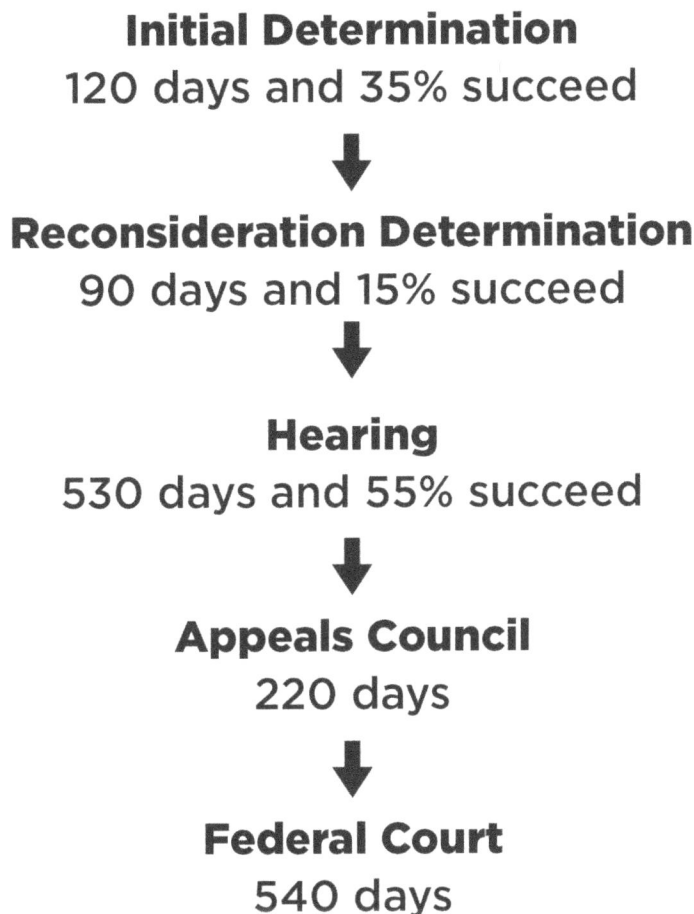

Initial Determination
120 days and 35% succeed

⬇

Reconsideration Determination
90 days and 15% succeed

⬇

Hearing
530 days and 55% succeed

⬇

Appeals Council
220 days

⬇

Federal Court
540 days

These are approximate national average completion times.

Source: https://www.pioneerlawoffice.com/social-security-disability-resources/

QUESTIONS:

Is the appeals process clear to you, or do you still have questions about it?

....

....

....

....

....

How big a discrepancy would have to exist between what you *expected* to receive and what the SSA *approves* for you to decide to use the appeals process? Would you do it for an extra $50 a month? $150? $500?

....

....

....

....

....

NOTES:

....

....

....

....

....

....

....

....

....

....

....

....

....

....

....

....

....

....

....

....

CLAIMING SURVIVORS BENEFITS

Survivors benefits are paid to widows, widowers, and dependents of eligible workers. If you are a worker who pays into Social Security, a portion of those taxes covers survivors benefits. In effect, this is a form of life insurance that can be worth hundreds of thousands of dollars to you.

Here are the steps to apply for survivors benefits:

- You should notify the SSA as soon as possible if someone dies. This cannot be done online. Call the national number at 1-800-772-1213 or contact your local SSA office. Visit https://PrepareforSocialSecurity.com for a wealth of resources to find your local SSA office, phone number, and driving directions.

- If you are receiving benefits based on your spouse's or parent's work record, you will not typically need to file an application, as the changes should happen automatically.

- If you are not already receiving Social Security benefits, you should apply right away for survivors benefits because the benefits may not be retroactive.

- Decide what types of benefits you want to apply for:

  ○ Widows/Widowers or Surviving Divorced Spouse's Benefits

  ○ Child's Benefits

  ○ Mother's or Father's Benefits

  ○ Lump-Sum Death Payment

  ○ Parent's Benefits (if you're dependent on your child at the time of his or her death)

- Visit this site to complete the necessary forms for the benefits you wish to apply for: https://PrepareforSocialSecurity.com/links.

- Collect and provide to the SSA the documents required to complete each type of benefit application. These can include proof of the worker's death, proof of your birth, proof of citizenship, tax returns, and marriage or divorce certificates.

Deceased DID NOT File for Benefits	Died BEFORE Full Retirement Age	Deceased's full retirement age benefit (adjusted for survivor's filing age)
	Died AFTER Full Retirement Age	Deceased's benefit if they would have filed on the day of death (adjusted for survivor's filing age)
Deceased DID File for Benefits	Filed ON or AFTER Full Retirement Age	Benefit amount deceased was receiving at death (adjusted for survivor's filing age)
	Filed BEFORE Full Retirement Age	Maximum Benefit: Actual benefit of the deceased *or* 82.5% of the deceased's FRA benefit (adjusted for survivor's filing age)

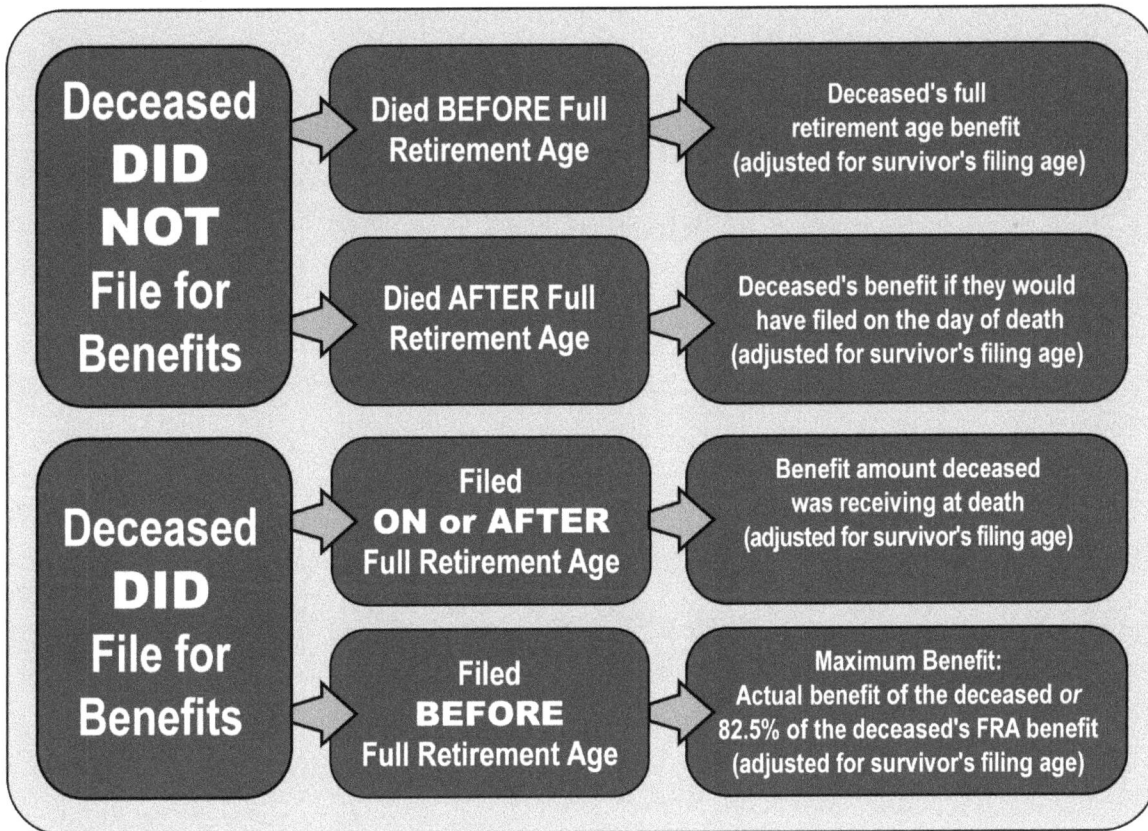

Source: https://www.socialsecurityintelligence.com/social-security-survivor-benefits-and-death/

QUESTIONS:

What type of survivors benefits might apply to you if a loved one passes away?

....

....

....

....

....

....

How can you make sure, if you pass away, your loved ones will know what survivors benefits they will be entitled to?

....

....

....

....

....

....

NOTES:

HOW TO FILE FOR BENEFITS

- Decide when you want your benefits to start, as early as 62, or as late as 70.

- File an application up to four months before the date you want your benefits to start. There are four ways you can file:

1. Complete a paper application, and mail or deliver it to an SSA office.

2. Complete an application at an SSA office with the help of an SSA representative.

3. Phone the SSA at 800-772-1213 to complete the application over the phone with a representative.

4. Open a *my Social Security* account on the SSA website and complete an online application.

Website: https://www.ssa.gov/

National Phone Number: 1-800-772-1213

Email: https://secure.ssa.gov/emailus/

Postal mail:

Social Security Administration

Office of Public Inquiries and Communications Support

1100 West High Rise

6401 Security Blvd.

Baltimore, MD 21235

Find local office by ZIP code: https://secure.ssa.gov/ICON/main.jsp

OR

https://www.PrepareforSocialSecurity.com

QUESTIONS:

Which method of filing for Social Security will be more efficient for you?

....

....

....

....

....

If you have difficulty working through the process, who is a trusted and knowledgeable family member or friend who can help you navigate the bureaucracy?

....

....

....

....

....

....

NOTES:

NAVIGATING THE SYSTEM

Navigating the Social Security system can be a challenge. Here is a list of suggestions to help you:

- Keep your records organized, with everything related to Social Security in the same place.

- Take careful notes on phone calls and office visits, including the dates of the conversations.

- Photocopy everything you mail to the SSA, and always attach your Social Security number to every document and letter you send.

- Do not send irreplaceable documents through the mail. Instead, hand-deliver them to a local Social Security office.

- Use the Social Security Administration website to find general answers to many questions, download forms, and get a rough idea of your eligibility and estimated benefits amounts.

- If you need assistance because of problems with the SSA or your own health issues, you may bring a companion with you when you meet with SSA representatives, and this person may also help you complete the application process.

- In the case of very difficult problems, especially with disability issues, hiring a lawyer who specializes in Social Security cases may be necessary.

- If you want to register a complaint with the Social Security Administration, feedback can be registered at the SSA website or on a comment card at an SSA office. For more serious issues, you can contact your local SSA office in person or in writing, write to the national SSA office, contact your congressional representative for assistance, or secure the services of an attorney.

SECTION FOUR:

PREPARE TO FILE— USING A CONSULTANT OR ADVISOR

In this section, we will guide you through the process of filing for Social Security if you are using a consultant or advisor.

SHOULD YOU HIRE A CONSULTANT?

The primary way to decide if you should hire a consultant is whether or not you feel comfortable with your ability to navigate the Social Security Administration. An enormous number of online resources and books is available to help you (such as the one you're reading!). It's also not hard to find someone who has recently retired or helped a loved one through the process who might be able to help you thanks to their experience. The SSA personnel themselves are available to answer your questions by phone or in person at an SSA office.

Nevertheless, it can be confusing and stressful, especially because your decisions have long-term ramifications and cannot always be reversed. Some people appreciate the peace of mind of knowing someone who specializes in this field who can help them make the best decisions.

Throughout our lives, we hire doctors, attorneys, computer specialists, mechanics, and other professionals to provide services and advice we are not skilled enough to provide for ourselves. Getting help with Social Security planning is no different. Even highly skilled financial advisors often consult other professionals in difficult situations or even for help with their own retirement planning. It isn't easy to separate emotion from our decisions when handling our money. An outside professional can look at our situation objectively and give us logical advice.

Here are a few practical reasons many people decide hiring a consultant is a good investment. They can help you:

- Understand the process clearly and simply.
- Investigate solutions for your unique situation.
- Understand the tax implications of your decision.
- Plan for medical and retirement expenses in ways you hadn't considered.
- Navigate the appeals process if you need to use it.
- Be aware of additional benefits you may have overlooked.

Without an advisor, you are on your own to make decisions about Social Security. You can use the calculators and free tools on the SSA website and other places. Still, ultimately you make the final decisions, which may or may not match up with what you calculated using online resources. Advisors and consultants often have extra experience, software, and programs to confirm your choices, which automatically run many of the numbers you have to input manually with the SSA website.

A short caveat: while a consultant or advisor can be a great asset, there are two instances when you may need to get help from an attorney. The first is if you need to appeal a determination. With the various steps and bureaucracy of that process and the levels of judges and courts, it is best to hire an attorney with experience in these sorts of claims. The second is when you are filing for Social Security disability.

What are the downsides of using a consultant or advisor? Only a few, but they are significant:

- They may be more skilled in some areas than others, but not always in the areas you need.
- They may not have any professional accreditation or enough experience.
- They may not be inclined to offer thorough services to those with less ability to pay for their time.

All this underscores the importance of doing your homework to find a reputable, honest professional rather than picking the first name you find online or in an advertisement.

Here's a checklist to help you decide whether the professional you're thinking of hiring is legitimate:

- ☐ Ask for recommendations from people you know and trust.
- ☐ Search the internet for professionals with strong qualifications, credentials, and testimonials.
- ☐ Interview them to verify the impressions you got from their website. Examples of the types of questions you might ask are:

  - How long has your company been in business? What is its history and philosophy?
  - What services do you offer for people planning for retirement?
  - What is your educational background?
  - What credentials, certifications, or affiliations do you have for providing financial advice? These are examples of reputable professional organizations:

    - ○ National Association of Registered Social Security Analysts Ltd. (NARSSA)
    - ○ National Association of Personal Finance Advisors (NAPFA)
    - ○ National Social Security Association (NSSA)

  - Do you have a fiduciary obligation? (In other words, are they legally responsible for acting in the client's best interests, even if they receive less money for doing so?)
  - Can you provide references from other financial professionals?

- ☐ Note these red flags and run the other way!

  - Does what they say about the basics of Social Security benefits line up with what you've learned in this book and other reliable sources, or is it radically different?
  - Ask what retirement planning software they use. If they use no software, or only free calculators online, they could be charging you for what you could do yourself.
  - Are they patient with your questions, or abrupt or rude? Don't allow anyone to rush you or disrespect you. There are plenty of others who provide better customer service.

Types of Qualified Retirement Planners
Certified Financial Planner (CFP) – This is a recognized expert in financial planning, taxes, insurance, estate planning, and retirement. A CFP has passed standardized exams, and has demonstrated experience and ethical integrity. They also have a fiduciary duty, which means they must make decisions with the client's best interests in mind.
Chartered Retirement Plans Specialist (CRPS) – This professional develops and manages retirement plans for businesses. They are required to complete 16 hours of continuing education every two years to maintain their status.
Retirement Income Certified Professional (RICP) – This is an expert in retirement income planning. To earn this designation, they must have three years of business experience and complete three courses with exams.
Chartered Retirement Planning Counselor (CRPC) – This professional concentrates on helping clients work through retirement-related problems. They must complete six courses before receiving the CRPC designation and 16 hours of continuing education every two years.

QUESTIONS:

What do you think? For you, would hiring a professional Social Security consultant or advisor be worth the investment?

....

....

....

....

....

Who do you know and trust who could help you make a wise decision about hiring a professional?

....

....

....

....

....

....

NOTES:

....

....

....

....

....

....

....

....

....

....

....

....

....

....

....

....

....

....

....

....

WHAT TO EXPECT AT YOUR APPOINTMENT

Here's a checklist of what to expect at your appointment with a Social Security professional:

- ☐ They may have paperwork for you to complete online before your appointment, or they may complete it with you during your visit.

- ☐ They should also tell you what documents to bring to your appointment. These may include documents about your earnings, investments, bank accounts, and other financial documents.

- ☐ They will ask a series of questions. If you complete this workbook and gather the necessary documents before your appointment, you'll be organized and good to go!

- ☐ Your advisor will explain how to file for Social Security. Sometimes they will do it with you, or for you.

- ☐ If your advisor is a financial planner or wealth manager who provides Social Security advice, they may try to give you a comprehensive financial analysis. This is, of course, optional. Share only what you're comfortable with.

- ☐ Don't hesitate to accept any free services you would find useful without feeling obligated to purchase paid services.

- ☐ If the financial analysis is not free, feel free to turn it down. If you get the sense they are pushing advice or products that aren't a good fit for you, find a different advisor.

- ☐ Determine in advance that you will not make any decisions to purchase financial products during your meeting. Just collect the information and go home to think about it before committing to anything besides the Social Security advice you came for.

QUESTIONS:

Do you think you would be interested in other financial planning services than only Social Security advice?

....

....

....

....

....

If not, write out the reasons you are *not* interested and take your list with you to review before you get talked into anything you don't want or need.

....

....

....

....

....

NOTES:

....
....
....
....
....
....
....
....
....
....
....
....
....
....
....
....
....
....
....
....
....
....

ADDITIONAL CONTACTS

FINANCIAL ADVISOR(S):

....

....

....

....

CPA OR TAX PROFESSIONALS:

....

....

....

....

MEDICARE INSURANCE AGENT:

....

....

PROPERTY OR CASUALTY INSURANCE AGENT:

....

....

....

ESTATE PLANNING CONTACTS:

....

....

....

....

BANKING INFORMATION:

....

....

....

....

LIFE INSURANCE POLICIES WITH UP-TO-DATE BENEFICIARIES:

....

....

....

....

LONG-TERM CARE INSURANCE POLICIES:

....

....

....

....

CHILDREN'S NAMES AND PHONE NUMBERS:

....

....

....

....

....

....

GRANDCHILDREN'S NAMES AND PHONE NUMBERS:

....

....

....

....

....

....

....

....

....

....

....

....

....

ADDITIONAL CONTACT NOTES:

....

....

....

....

....

....

....

....

....

....

....

....

....

....

....

....

....

....

....

....

....

ADDITIONAL NOTES:

ADDITIONAL NOTES:

ADDITIONAL NOTES:

....

....

....

....

....

....

....

....

....

....

....

....

....

....

....

....

....

....

....

....

....

ADDITIONAL NOTES:

ADDITIONAL NOTES:

....

....

....

....

....

....

....

....

....

....

....

....

....

....

....

....

....

....

....

....

ADDITIONAL NOTES:

ADDITIONAL NOTES:

ADDITIONAL NOTES:

WHO IS MATT FERET?

Matt Feret is an author, educator, and longtime Medicare and Social Security insider. He creates books, workbooks, videos, and courses that help adults, retirees, and caregivers make confident financial and healthcare decisions.

Matt is the author of *Prepare for Social Security – The Insider's Guide*® and *Prepare for Medicare – The Insider's Guide*®, and host of *The Matt Feret Show*, which focuses on health, wealth, and wellness in midlife and beyond.

Company Name:

> MF Media, LLC

Email:

> mf@mattferet.com

Websites:

> https://PrepareforMedicare.com
>
> https://PrepareforSocialSecurity.com
>
> https://TheMattFeretShow.com

LinkedIn:

> linkedin.com/in/mattferet

Facebook:

> https://www.facebook.com/PrepareforMedicare

More Books by Matt Feret:

> https://www.amazon.com/author/mattferet

www.ingramcontent.com/pod-product-compliance
Lightning Source LLC
Chambersburg PA
CBHW080134240326

41458CB00128B/6449